LSAT®

PrepTest 83

Unlocked

Exclusive Data, Analysis, & Explanations for the December 2017 LSAT

PUBLISHING

New York

LSAT® is a registered mark of the Law School Admission Council, Inc.

© 2018 by Kaplan, Inc.

Published by Kaplan Publishing, a division of Kaplan, Inc.
750 Third Avenue
New York, NY 10017

ISBN: 978-1-5062-3765-7
10 9 8 7 6 5 4 3 2 1

Table of Contents

The Inside Story

PrepTest 83 was administered in December 2017. It challenged 40,096 test takers. What made this test so hard? Here's a breakdown of what Kaplan students who were surveyed after taking the official exam considered PrepTest 83's most difficult section.

Hardest PrepTest 83 Section as Reported by Test Takers

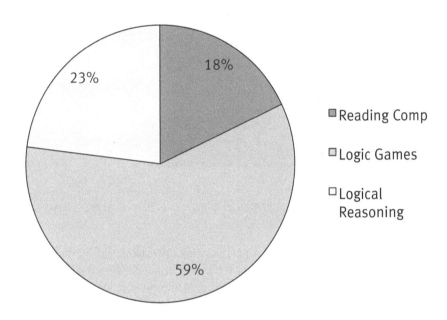

Based on these results, you might think that studying Logic Games is the key to LSAT success. Well, Logic Games is important, but test takers' perceptions don't tell the whole story. For that, you need to consider students' actual performance. The following chart shows the average number of students to miss each question in each of PrepTest 83's different sections.

Percentage Incorrect by PrepTest 83 Section Type

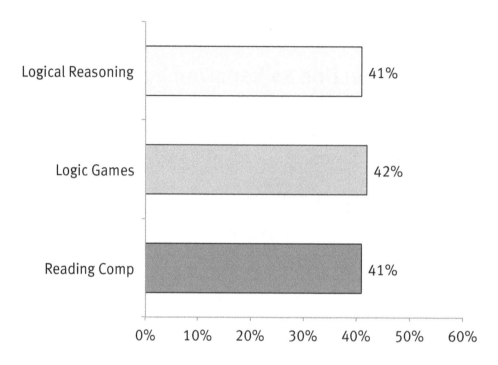

Actual student performance tells quite a different story. On average, students were almost equally likely to miss questions in all three of the different section types. Although Logic Games was somewhat higher in actual difficulty than Logical Reasoning and Reading Comprehension, because the Logic Games section has fewer questions than the other sections, that means the fewest incorrect answers came from the Logic Games section.

Maybe students overestimate the difficulty of the Logic Games section because it's so unusual, or maybe it's because a really hard Logic Game is so easy to remember after the test. The truth is that the testmaker places hard questions throughout the test. Here were the locations of the 10 hardest (most missed) questions in the exam.

Location of 10 Most Difficult Questions in PrepTest 83

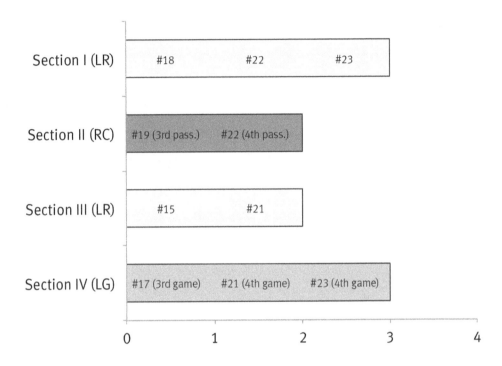

The takeaway from this data is that, to maximize your potential on the LSAT, you need to take a comprehensive approach. Test yourself rigorously, and review your performance on every section of the test. Kaplan's LSAT explanations provide the expertise and insight you need to fully understand your results. The explanations are written and edited by a team of LSAT experts, who have helped thousands of students improve their scores. Kaplan always provides data-driven analysis of the test, ranking the difficulty of every question based on actual student performance. The 10 hardest questions on every test are highlighted with a 4-star difficulty rating, the highest we give. The analysis breaks down the remaining questions into 1-, 2-, and 3-star ratings so that you can compare your performance to thousands of other test takers on all LSAC material.

Don't settle for wondering whether a question was really as hard as it seemed to you. Analyze the test with real data, and learn the secrets and strategies that help top scorers master the LSAT.

7 Can't-Miss Features of PrepTest 83

- With 10 Assumption questions, PT 83 was only the third test since 2010 with 10 or more on a single LSAT. The two other times this happened were October 2015 (PT 76) and September 2016 (PT 79).
- This was the second PrepTest since June 2002 (PT 37) with no Main Point questions. The other test was October 2015 (PT 76).
- PT 83 tied the all-time record for most Point at Issue questions at five. The only other test to have five was in February 2000 (PT C).
- PT 83 featured a Selection game for only the third time in the last six years. There was also one in October 2013 (PT 70) and June 2016 (PT 78).
- The Logic Games section has only started with a Hybrid game nine times ever. That said, PT 83 was the third consecutive test to do so! A new trend?
- Another new trend? It's unusual for the Comparative Reading set of passages to have eight questions, but for just the third time since December 2009 (PT 59), this test's Comparative Reading passages were accompanied by eight questions. That also makes it two tests in a row on which that has happened.

- Yet another new trend? For the second consecutive test, the LSAC eschewed a Humanities passage in favor of a second Social Science passage.

PrepTest 83 in Context

As much fun as it is to find out what makes a PrepTest unique or noteworthy, it's even more important to know just how representative it is of other LSAT administrations (and, thus, how likely it is to be representative of the exam you will face on Test Day). The following charts compare the numbers of each kind of question and game on PrepTest 83 to the average numbers seen on all officially released LSATs administered over the past five years (from 2013 through 2017).

Number of LR Questions by Type: PrepTest 83 vs. 2013–2017 Average

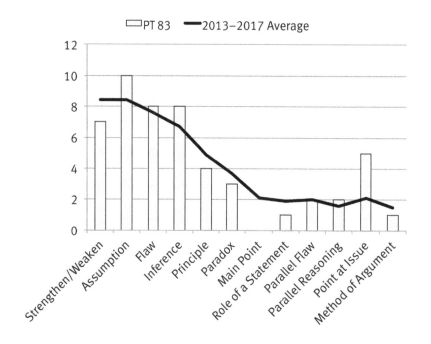

Number of LG Games by Type: PrepTest 83 vs. 2013–2017 Average

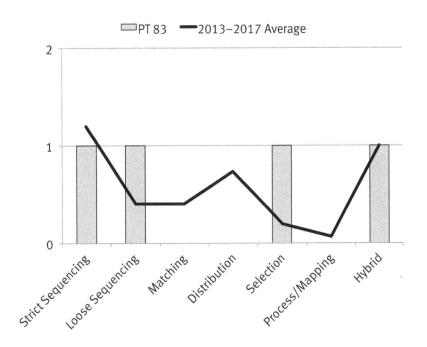

Number of RC Questions by Type: PrepTest 83 vs. 2013–2017 Average

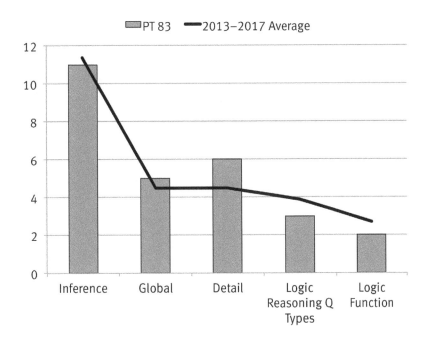

There isn't usually a huge difference in the distribution of questions from LSAT to LSAT, but if this test seems harder (or easier) to you than another you've taken, compare the number of questions of the types on which you, personally, are strongest and weakest. Then, explore within each section to see if your best or worst question types came earlier or later.

Students in Kaplan's comprehensive LSAT courses have access to every released LSAT and to a library of thousands of officially released questions arranged by question, game, and passage type. If you are studying on your own, you have to do a bit more work to identify your strengths and your areas of opportunity. Quantitative analysis (like that in the charts shown here) is an important tool for understanding how the test is constructed, and how you are performing on it.

Section I: Logical Reasoning

Q#	Question Type	Correct	Difficulty
1	Weaken	C	★
2	Flaw	D	★
3	Point at Issue	A	★
4	Flaw	C	★★
5	Strengthen	C	★
6	Parallel Flaw	D	★
7	Point at Issue	A	★
8	Method of Argument	E	★
9	Principle (Identify/Strengthen)	A	★★★
10	Paradox	C	★★
11	Inference	A	★
12	Flaw	A	★★
13	Inference	C	★★★
14	Assumption (Necessary)	B	★★
15	Inference	E	★
16	Flaw	C	★★★
17	Assumption (Necessary)	B	★
18	Inference	E	★★★★
19	Paradox	A	★★
20	Principle (Identify/Strengthen)	D	★★★
21	Assumption (Necessary)	B	★★★
22	Flaw	A	★★★★
23	Strengthen	C	★★★★
24	Assumption (Sufficient)	B	★★
25	Parallel Reasoning	C	★★

1. (C) Weaken

Step 1: Identify the Question Type
The question asks for something that "weakens the argument," making this a Weaken question.

Step 2: Untangle the Stimulus
The author concludes ([*t*]*hus*) that Chu will likely defeat Lewis in the mayoral race. The evidence is that Chu is prodevelopment, Lewis is not, and the last six mayoral winners have been prodevelopment.

Step 3: Make a Prediction
The author uses past performance to predict what will happen in the next election. However, predictions like this assume there will be no significant change that could affect the future results. Here, the author assumes voters will continue to be prodevelopment. To weaken this argument, the correct choice will provide a reason why people might want to buck the trend and no longer support development.

Step 4: Evaluate the Answer Choices
(C) is correct. This suggests that voters may now have problems with development that didn't exist previously (they're *new* problems). In that case, it's not as convincing that they'd continue their trend of choosing the prodevelopment candidate.

(A) is a 180. The lack of experience in city politics could just add another reason why voters would not vote for Lewis.

(B) is a 180. If prodevelopment candidates, such as Chu, attract more financial backing, that suggests they have greater support, making it appear that Chu does have a better chance.

(D) is Out of Scope. It doesn't matter what views were held by someone Lewis worked for. If people want development and Lewis is personally anti-development, then that works against Lewis, as the author predicts.

(E) is Out of Scope. All that matters is that voters recognize Chu as prodevelopment now. If that's true, that gives Chu an advantage based on past voting results.

2. (D) Flaw

Step 1: Identify the Question Type
The question asks for an expression that was *misinterpreted*, which indicates a Flaw in the reasoning.

Step 2: Untangle the Stimulus
Rose doesn't want to see a movie called *Winter Fields* because she claims the local paper gave it one of the worst reviews she's seen in years. Chester refutes Rose's reasoning by arguing that nothing in the local paper is well written.

Step 3: Make a Prediction
The problem here is that Chester's argument rests on the quality of the writing in the local paper. When Rose claims the review was one of the *worst* she read, she was referring to the critical content of the review, not the poor writing style. So, Chester's error rests in his misinterpretation of what Rose meant by the "worst review."

Step 4: Evaluate the Answer Choices
(D) is correct.

(A) is incorrect. When Rose says "see the movie," she means going to the theater and watching the movie, and Chester interprets that properly.

(B) is incorrect. When Rose says "caught a review," it means she saw it in the local paper. Chester makes no mistake in interpreting that.

(C) is incorrect. The "local paper" is used consistently by both speakers to refer to a particular newspaper.

(E) is incorrect. Chester does not misinterpret the length of time between bad reviews seen by Rose.

3. (A) Point at Issue

Step 1: Identify the Question Type
The question asks for something about which two speakers *disagree*, making this a Point at Issue question.

Step 2: Untangle the Stimulus
Enrique argues that the transit authority, which will run out of funds within 12 months, should not cut services or raise fares and should instead continue current operations until the funds run out. This is based on the belief that, when the funds do run out, the government will step in to save the authority. Cynthia argues otherwise, claiming that the government will probably not step in and will instead let the authority shut down. Thus, she argues that the transit authority should not take that risk.

Step 3: Make a Prediction
There are two issues being debated. The first is the question of what the government would do if the funds run out. Would it step in and save the authority or let the authority go out of business? And this serves as the basis for the other debate: Should the authority take a gamble and let the funds run out to see what happens? The correct answer will address one of these two debates.

Step 4: Evaluate the Answer Choices
(A) is correct. Enrique agrees with this claim, arguing that the authority should take such measures. Cynthia disagrees, claiming the authority cannot take the risk.

(B) is a Distortion. The debate is about whether the government *will* provide funding, not whether it *should*. It's possible they both agree that the government should help, regardless of whether or not it actually does.

(C) is an Irrelevant Comparison. Neither Enrique nor Cynthia make any claims about which alternative, cutting services or raising fares, would be better for the authority. The debate is about doing either alternative versus doing neither of them.

(D) is likely a 180. Enrique claims the government has failed to provide funding thus far, suggesting that the government is currently unwilling to do so. And if Cynthia believes the government would be willing to let the authority go out of business, that suggests she would *agree* about the government's reluctance.

(E) is likely also a 180. Enrique clearly rejects this claim, saying that the authority cannot afford to maintain operations. Cynthia does not comment directly on the subject, but her claim that the authority cannot risk going out of business suggests she agrees with Enrique about the authority's financial situation.

4. (C) Flaw

Step 1: Identify the Question Type
The question asks why the reasoning provided is questionable, making this a Flaw question.

Step 2: Untangle the Stimulus
The author argues that aerobic exercise has a beneficial effect on people's health. The evidence is a survey (confirmed by other surveys) showing that people who exercise more tend to have less risk of lung disease.

Step 3: Make a Prediction
The evidence provides a correlation (people who exercise have lower risk of lung disease), but the author is suggesting that the exercise is responsible for the lower risk of lung disease. This is a commonly tested flaw in which the author confuses a correlation for causation. The lower risk of lung disease could be caused by other factors, the causation could be reversed (i.e., people with healthy lungs are able to exercise more), or the statistics could just be coincidental. The correct answer will describe this common flaw.

Step 4: Evaluate the Answer Choices
(C) is correct. Exercise and low risk of lung disease are merely correlated, but that doesn't mean the author can conclude that one caused the other.

(A) is not a flaw. If the scientific results are substantial, then there's no need for anecdotal evidence.

(B) is a 180. The author also refers to other surveys that confirm the results of the medical journal survey.

(D) is a Distortion. The author's conclusion is not that people are healthy ("in good health"). The author is merely arguing that there was a beneficial effect, even if that one effect is negated by other problems.

(E) is a 180, at worst. The survey results show that the more people exercise, the lower their risk of lung disease. That suggests that even a little exercise could have *some* effect, and there's no indication that the author fails to notice this.

5. (C) Strengthen

Step 1: Identify the Question Type
The question directly asks for something that strengthens the given argument.

Step 2: Untangle the Stimulus
The researchers conclude that a particular genetic defect leads to a greater risk of herniated disks. The evidence is that, in a study, 5 of the 100 people with herniated disks had the genetic defect while none of the 100 people without disk problems had the defect.

Step 3: Make a Prediction
It's interesting that all five people in the study with the genetic defect happened to have herniated disks. However, the author is still confusing correlation and causation. In other words, the author is assuming that it's not just a coincidence and that the defect does, in fact, play a causal role in people getting herniated disks. With such a small sample size in the study, it would help the author to have additional data connecting the genetic defect to herniated disks.

Step 4: Evaluate the Answer Choices
(C) is correct. This would provide 30 more people with the defective gene, all with herniated disks. This suggests a stronger correlation between the gene and herniated disks, making it more likely that the gene plays some role in the problem.

(A) is a 180. The people in this survey don't have the gene and are still getting herniated disks. This makes no connection between the gene and the disks, and could even suggest they're ultimately unrelated.

(B) is a 180. This suggests that the five people in the original study may have been anomalies, as only 2% of these people with the gene get herniated disks. That implies the gene has very little, if any, impact on herniated disks.

(D) is a 180. If none of these people had the defective genes, then there is no additional evidence that the gene plays any role in people getting herniated disks.

(E) is a 180. This just provides evidence of more people who get herniated disks without the defective gene. This fails to provide any link between the gene and herniated disks.

6. (D) Parallel Flaw

Step 1: Identify the Question Type
The correct answer will have reasoning *parallel* to that in the stimulus, and that reasoning is said to be *flawed*, making this a Parallel Flaw question.

Step 2: Untangle the Stimulus
The evidence is Formal Logic, claiming that the only vehicles with high resale values are those that are well maintained. In other words, if a vehicle has a high resale value, it must be

well maintained. The author then concludes (/t/hus) that all well-maintained vehicles have a high resale value.

If	**high resale value**	→	**well maintained**

If	**well maintained**	→	**high resale value**

Step 3: Make a Prediction

The author is confusing sufficiency and necessity. Good maintenance is presented as necessary for a high resale value, but it's not sufficient. In other words, there could be plenty of well maintained cars that do *not* have high resale values. The correct answer will be an argument that commits the same flaw: identifies a trait (well maintained) common to items in one group (vehicles with high resale value) and tries to conclude that *all* items with that trait are part of the group.

Step 4: Evaluate the Answer Choices

(D) matches. The author identifies a trait (preference for waterfalls over traffic) common to people in one group (city dwellers) and tries to conclude that *all* people with that trait belong to the group. Just like the original argument, this ignores the possibility that there are plenty of people who prefer waterfalls yet do *not* live in the city.

If	**city dweller**	→	**waterfalls > traffic jams**

If	**waterfalls > traffic jams**	→	**city dweller**

(A) does not match. This makes an illicit shift from what's happened in the past to what needs to be done in the present, but the original argument makes no such temporal shift.

(B) does not match. This makes an illogical deduction that what's true of the best people in a field must be the complete opposite of what's true for the worst people in that field. The original argument presents no such dichotomy.

(C) does not match. This commits a flaw of saying one attribute common to all members of a group must be the "most important" attribute. The original argument never identified any trait as the most important.

(E) does not match. This presents an inverse proportion: As health improves, need for medical care decreases. The original argument did not describe any such proportional relationship.

7. (A) Point at Issue

Step 1: Identify the Question Type

The question asks for something about which two speakers *disagree*, making this a Point at Issue question.

Step 2: Untangle the Stimulus

Rita argues that the survey results in question are misleading, no matter how they're interpreted. Her evidence is that people lie, and thus the collected numbers are underestimates. Hiro admits that people can lie on surveys and that the numbers may be underestimates, but argues that the relative rates can still be seen as accurate.

Step 3: Make a Prediction

Hiro admits that the survey results aren't perfect. However, unlike Rita, Hiro sees at least one way to get accurate information out of the survey: look at the relative rates. Rita says otherwise: The numbers are inaccurate no matter what. So, the point at issue is whether or not there is *some* way to glean accurate information from the survey.

Step 4: Evaluate the Answer Choices

(A) is correct. Rita would agree with this, saying the results are inevitably misleading. Hiro would disagree, saying the results are not misleading if you interpret the relative rates.

(B) is a 180. Both speakers claim, and thus agree, that people lie on surveys.

(C) is Out of Scope. Neither speaker mentions methods other than the survey in question.

(D) is a 180. Hiro does not dispute this claim by Rita. In fact, Hiro admits that the raw numbers are surely underestimates.

(E) is Out of Scope. Neither speaker discusses or questions the number of people who were surveyed.

8. (E) Method of Argument

Step 1: Identify the Question Type

The question asks how Warrington's argument *proceeds*, making this a Method of Argument question.

Step 2: Untangle the Stimulus

Lopez argues that the university is not committed to liberal arts. As evidence, Lopez cites the closing of the classics department, which would deny students a subject crucial to liberal arts. Warrington admits that studying classical works is essential, but points out that there are other departments that provide that necessary study.

Step 3: Make a Prediction

Lopez assumes that the classics department was the only place to study classical works. Warrington refutes that assumption by pointing out an overlooked alternative: Students can learn about the classics in other departments, so there's no reason to suggest the university is unconcerned with liberal arts. The correct answer will describe Warrington's approach of questioning Lopez by raising overlooked alternatives.

Step 4: Evaluate the Answer Choices

(E) is correct. Warrington presents a consideration that classical works can be taught elsewhere, thus undermining Lopez's argument.

(A) is a 180. Warrington is rejecting Lopez's argument, not favoring it.

(B) is a Distortion. Lopez does appeal to tradition (studying classics has been crucial since the Renaissance), but Warrington does not address or question that claim. Instead, Warrington questions a different assumption about whether a classics department is needed to study classical works.

(C) is a Distortion. Warrington never directly states that Lopez is wrong or directly claims that the university *is* committed to liberal arts. Instead, Warrington questions Lopez's assumption and thus *indirectly* challenges Lopez's argument.

(D) is a Distortion. Warrington does not respond to a possible objection. Warrington presents that objection personally.

9. (A) Principle (Identify/Strengthen)

Step 1: Identify the Question Type
The question directly asks for a principle, and one that will "help to justify" an argument, making this an Identify the Principle question that works like a Strengthen question.

Step 2: Untangle the Stimulus
The question asks about Tatiana's decision, which comes at the end: She doesn't request a replacement for Ted. Although he intentionally works fewer hours, causing other workers to pick up the slack, it is also noted that Ted is valuable, making "unique and perhaps irreplaceable contributions."

Step 3: Make a Prediction
Ted's work ethic is certainly questionable, so why not replace him? It would appear Tatiana is swayed by Ted's invaluable contributions. She is acting on the principle that, even if they skimp on hours, employees should not be replaced if they can make superior contributions.

Step 4: Evaluate the Answer Choices
(A) is correct. Translating the Formal Logic here, if a supervisor wants to request a replacement, the supervisor must be sure that the employee's work can be done equally well by somebody else.

$$\text{If} \quad \textbf{replacement} \quad \rightarrow \quad \begin{array}{l} \textbf{work can be} \\ \textbf{done equally} \\ \textbf{well by} \\ \textbf{somebody else} \end{array}$$

By contrapositive, if that employee's work cannot be done equally well by others (like Ted's unique and irreplaceable contributions), then the supervisor should not request a replacement, as Tatiana decides.

$$\text{If} \quad \begin{array}{l} \textbf{work can $\sim$ be} \\ \textbf{done equally} \\ \textbf{well by} \\ \textbf{somebody else} \end{array} \quad \rightarrow \quad \textbf{$\sim$ replacement}$$

(B) is Out of Scope. Tatiana's decision has nothing to do with compensation.

(C) is Extreme. If *only* people above Tatiana (Ted's supervisor's supervisor or higher (e.g., Tatiana's boss)) have the authority to decide whether Ted should be replaced, then there's no decision for Tatiana to make at all, so her reasoning would not be justified. Tatiana *does* have the authority to replace Ted—she just chooses not to do so.

(D) is Out of Scope. There's no question about responsibility here, and this offers no justification for whether Ted should be replaced or not.

(E) is irrelevant. While this may be a valid observation based on Ted's performance, this has no bearing on Tatiana's decision regarding Ted's replacement.

10. (C) Paradox

Step 1: Identify the Question Type
The correct answer will provide a "resolution of the apparent discrepancy mentioned," making this a Paradox question.

Step 2: Untangle the Stimulus
The author notes that camouflage is an effective adaptation for surviving in the face of predators. *Yet*, the author also notes that some animals have escaped predation despite being just black and white and having no other useful adaptations against predators.

Step 3: Make a Prediction
As with any Paradox question, start by paraphrasing the mystery at hand. In this case, how are black-and-white animals able to avoid predators when they have no other adaptations against predators? There must be something about the black-and-white coloration, no matter how unlikely, that makes it effective. Don't bother predicting something specific. Instead, look for an answer that provides some reason why that bold coloring doesn't reduce its effectiveness.

Step 4: Evaluate the Answer Choices
(C) is correct. This suggests that, while black and white may seem to stand out to us, other predatory animals don't see colors the same way. So, perhaps the black-and-white pattern

blends into the background for predators, giving the black-and-white animals the protection they need to survive.

(A) is irrelevant. Even if black-and-white animals have large populations, that doesn't explain why they're not being attacked by predators.

(B) is Extreme. Even if there's no perfect camouflage, this offers no explanation how black-and-white animals are so effective at avoiding predators.

(D) is irrelevant. The paradox is about how black-and-white animals avoid predators, not contact with each other. If anything, this states that black-and-white areas are conspicuous (i.e., they stand out more). That only deepens the mystery, making it even stranger that they've effectively avoided predators.

(E) is an Irrelevant Comparison, and a 180 at worst. This just suggests that black-and-white coloration isn't as much of a problem at night. However, if it's still a problem during the day, then the mystery is unresolved: How are they avoiding predators?

11. (A) Inference
Step 1: Identify the Question Type
The question asks for a claim that the given statements "most strongly support." That means the correct answer will be an Inference based on the statements provided.

Step 2: Untangle the Stimulus
The lecturer is discussing an interesting discrepancy. The phrase "I tried to get my work done on time" does not actually state the work wasn't finished, but that's what people would correctly think it means. If the work was done on time, you'd say "I got the work done on time." The lecturer claims this is a typical example of how conversation works.

Step 3: Make a Prediction
The lecturer makes an interesting point. When we say we *tried* to do something, we often mean that we failed, even though we don't say it. Yet, people understand that without you having to explain it. It serves to show that people can understand your intention, even if your words don't explicitly say it. The correct answer will be consistent with this idea.

Step 4: Evaluate the Answer Choices
(A) is correct. Using the lecturer's phrase as an example, the word *tried* means "made an attempt," which does not indicate success or failure. To understand the meaning (that the speaker failed), you have to understand why that word was used, not just the word's definition. And the lecturer calls the given example *typical*, which supports that this *often* happens. (*Often* is not extreme, as it's merely a relative term.)

(B) is a 180. The lecturer cites the example of *tried* as typical, which suggests it is not unusual.

(C) is Out of Scope. There is no indication of using nonverbal cues.

(D) is a Distortion. The idea is that our conversation provides information beyond the words themselves. However, we expect people to understand that information, so it is exactly what we intend, not more than what we intend.

(E) is a 180. In the lecturer's example, it's anticipated that the listener "would correctly understand" the meaning. That suggests the listener *does* indeed have what's needed to communicate successfully.

12. (A) Flaw
Step 1: Identify the Question Type
The question asks why the argument provided is "most vulnerable to criticism," commonly used language to indicate there's a Flaw in the argument.

Step 2: Untangle the Stimulus
The legislator concludes that the new highway bill is unpopular. The evidence is that many members of the party that supported the bill will lose their seats in the upcoming election.

Step 3: Make a Prediction
The legislator assumes that the party members in question are being ousted because of their support of the highway bill. However, voters might love the highway bill but have countless other reasons to vote out those party members. Maybe there was a scandal. Maybe the party members passed a completely different bill that was highly unpopular. Maybe voters just want a change and want to elect some new people. The decision could have nothing to do with the highway bill, and the correct answer will address this flaw of overlooked possibilities.

Step 4: Evaluate the Answer Choices
(A) is correct. If the majority party was going to be voted out regardless, then the highway bill would be irrelevant. The bill might still be popular, and voters could have other reasons to vote the majority party out. And that's what the legislator completely overlooks.

(B) is not a flaw. Yes, the legislator does focus solely on the bill's popularity, but that's the point of the argument. The question of merit is an entirely different argument, and the legislator has no need to discuss that here.

(C) describes the flaw of Circular Reasoning, but that's not happening here. The support for the legislator's conclusion is poll results. Poll results are merely statistics based on people's responses to a survey. Statistics cannot presuppose anything.

(D) is Out of Scope. The legislator offers no personal opinion on the bill, so there's no evidence that the legislator wishes the bill to be unpopular. It's equally likely the legislator is disappointed by the unpopularity.

(E) is Out of Scope. The argument is solely about popularity. It doesn't matter if voters have no expertise. The argument is not about the merit of the bill or whether voters are justified in their judgment.

13. (C) Inference

Step 1: Identify the Question Type
The question asks for something that "must be true" based on the statements given, making this an Inference question.

Step 2: Untangle the Stimulus
Songwriters make money from having their song played on the radio. Hit songs are played thousands of times, earning money for the songwriter every time. However, it's relatively uncommon for songwriters to write a hit song, let alone multiple ones. The author then discusses songs on movie sound tracks. Many of these songs become hit songs, but some songwriters avoid writing such songs because they only receive a one-time payment for those songs.

Step 3: Make a Prediction
A lot of the information is about *some* songs and *some* songwriters. The most concrete piece of information is about hit songs, which are played thousands of times and make songwriters money *each* time they're played. Only some songwriters write such songs, but each of those songs will make money and be played thousands of times. And some songs on movie sound tracks become hits, so those songs will also be played thousands of times. Beyond that, there's not a lot to work with here. Instead of predicting a specific deduction, be on the lookout for Extreme choices and make sure the correct answer is absolutely supported.

Step 4: Evaluate the Answer Choices
(C) must be true. It is said that sound track songs "frequently become hits," and hit songs are "played thousand of times." So, logically, there are definitely sound track songs that become hits and are played thousands of times.

(A) is Extreme. Hit songs do produce revenue for each play, but they're not necessarily the *only* songs that do so. Songwriters might also receive revenue for minor songs played only a few hundred times.

(B) is Extreme. Sound track songs are said to *frequently* become hits, but that doesn't mean it always happens, and not necessarily for every songwriter that tries.

(D) is Extreme. Songwriters are said to *sometimes* decline writing songs for sound tracks because of the up-front payment method. However, that doesn't mean *most* songwriters act this way. Most songwriters might be fine with the up-front payment.

(E) is Extreme. The first sentence says songwriters get *much* of their money from radio airplay of their songs, but there's no suggestion that airplay is the *sole* source of income for any songwriters.

14. (B) Assumption (Necessary)

Step 1: Identify the Question Type
The question directly asks for an assumption, and one on which the argument *depends*, making this a Necessary Assumption question.

Step 2: Untangle the Stimulus
The debate coach is arguing that Robert's performance was just as good as Britta's. The evidence is that, although Britta had better command of historical facts, it's also important to consider how reasonable the arguments were.

Step 3: Make a Prediction
If Britta has better command of historical facts, how did Robert perform equally well overall? He must have compensated elsewhere. The only other factor mentioned is reasonability, but the coach never actually states how Robert did with reasonability. To call Robert and Britta even, the coach must assume that Robert outperformed Britta in reasonability.

Step 4: Evaluate the Answer Choices
(B) must be assumed. Using the Denial Test, if Robert's arguments were *not* more reasonable, then Britta would be just as good or better, and she also had better command of historical facts. There would be no basis for judging Robert as equal. Robert's arguments had to be more reasonable to claim otherwise.

(A) is not necessary. Britta didn't have to be entirely *unreasonable*. She could have had very reasonable arguments, but Robert's could still have been even better.

(C) is Extreme. Reasonability is an important factor to evaluate, but a good debate doesn't have to have *very* reasonable arguments. Even if the arguments are mildly reasonable, there could be enough to compensate and call the debates *good*.

(D) is Extreme. The argument is about comparing who did better. Neither speaker had to be in *full* command of the facts. In fact, Britta's command was better, so it's possible she did have full command and only Robert slipped up a little.

(E) is not necessary. Britta had the better command of facts, yet Robert is still said to be equally good overall, and so may still win the debate. Besides, winning may not be about having good command, per se. They could have both had a terrible command of the facts, but one would still win by being just a little less terrible.

15. (E) Inference

Step 1: Identify the Question Type
The correct answer will be "strongly supported by the information" provided, which means it will be an inference based on the author's statements.

Step 2: Untangle the Stimulus
The author describes how physicists try to create new atoms by fusing two other atoms together. To do this, physicists make the two atoms collide. Atoms try to repel one another, so the collision requires enough energy to overcome that (i.e., the atoms have to move really, really fast). However, it has to be relatively precise. If there's too much energy (i.e., the atoms move too fast), the excess energy turns into heat. If the new atom is too hot, it will just break apart immediately.

Step 3: Make a Prediction
It might seem like you need a degree in nuclear physics to understand all of this, but don't let the big sciency words scare you. Simply put: Take two thingies, then smash them together with enough energy, and voila—you get a new thingie. But be careful. Too much energy, and your new thingie will get too hot and break apart. The correct answer will adhere to this logic without distorting it or bringing in new information.

Step 4: Evaluate the Answer Choices
(E) is supported. If there is considerably more energy than is needed, then the new atom will be very hot, which is a condition said to increase the chance of immediate breakdown.

(A) is not supported. Splitting apart is said to happen when the new atom gets too hot (perhaps from too much energy), but there's no indication that this is *usually* what happens.

(B) is a 180. The last sentence suggests that the new atom can split apart when there is too much energy, not when there's too little energy.

(C) is a 180. The new atom is said to be hot when there is *excess* energy in the collision. If the amount of energy is just the right amount to overcome the electromagnetic force, then the temperature need not be hot regardless of how much force had to be overcome.

(D) is not supported. If a new atom is formed and it doesn't fall apart, then little *excess* energy is produced. However, the collision could still have produced a lot of energy from the fusion in the first place, even if the new atom doesn't fall apart. So, the collision may have created a lot of energy, just not enough *excess* energy that converted into heat to cause the atom to split.

16. (C) Flaw

Step 1: Identify the Question Type
The question asks why an "argument is flawed," making this a Flaw question.

Step 2: Untangle the Stimulus
Fremont argues that Simpson shouldn't be chief executive of Pod Oil due to a lack of experience in the oil industry. Galindo disagrees, essentially concluding that Simpson is still a viable candidate. As evidence, Galindo refers to the previous executive who did a terrible job despite having decades of experience.

Step 3: Make a Prediction
The previous executive's performance makes it clear that experience is no guarantee of success. However, Fremont is not arguing that experience *will* guarantee success (i.e., that experience is sufficient). Fremont is merely suggesting that a *lack* of experience is *not* good (i.e., experience is necessary). Even if experience isn't enough by itself, as Galindo claims, it still might be an important component, and Galindo overlooks that.

Step 4: Evaluate the Answer Choices
(C) is correct. Fremont is suggesting that experience is necessary, and Galindo's argument rests on showing how experience is not sufficient. However, even if experience is not sufficient, it could still be necessary, and Simpson could still be a poor candidate.

(A) is Out of Scope. There is no accusation toward Fremont for bias.

(B) is Out of Scope. Both speakers refer to background in the oil industry, i.e., relevant experience. There is no irrelevant experience to distinguish.

(D) is a Distortion. Galindo is not saying experience is irrelevant. Galindo is merely claiming that it's not enough, even if it is relevant.

(E) is a Distortion. Galindo does use evidence of a single event (the previous executive) to properly make a broad generalization ("[a]n oil industry background is no guarantee of success"). However, the flaw is that using that single event does not adequately address Fremont's claim that experience is necessary.

17. (B) Assumption (Necessary)

Step 1: Identify the Question Type
The question asks for an assumption, and one that is "required by the argument," making this a Necessary Assumption question.

Step 2: Untangle the Stimulus
The author concludes ([*h*]*ence*) that lightning discharge data can sometimes be the only way to measure the altitude of ash

clouds. The evidence is that weather radar can be used in some areas, but it's not available everywhere in the world.

Step 3: Make a Prediction

If an area has weather radar that can measure the altitude, then lightning discharge would not be the *only* reliable indicator in that area. For lightning discharge to be the only reliable indicator, it would have to be found in areas without weather radar. However, there's no evidence that lightning discharge can be found in such areas. For this argument to work, the author must assume that lightning discharge *can* be found in areas with no weather radar.

Step 4: Evaluate the Answer Choices

(B) is correct. By the Denial Test, if lightning discharges *cannot* be detected in such areas, then they are only detected in areas that *do* have weather radar. In that case, they will never be the only reliable indicator of altitude. To argue otherwise, the author must believe that lightning discharges *can* be found elsewhere.

(A) is Extreme. It doesn't have to be the case that *all* ash clouds reach 5 km or higher. Even if there are some ash clouds that don't reach that altitude, the author could still have a point that lightning discharge is the only reliable indicator in some areas where they do reach that altitude.

(C) is an Irrelevant Comparison. The argument is solely about measuring the altitude of ash clouds. It doesn't matter how much better or worse radar is at measuring altitude of other types of clouds.

(D) is irrelevant. Even if nothing is beyond the reach of weather radar, the author could still have a point about using lightning discharge data in areas that don't have weather radar at all.

(E) is an Irrelevant Comparison. The argument is about measuring the altitude of ash clouds, not their comparative size or the frequency of lightning discharges.

18. (E) Inference

Step 1: Identify the Question Type

The question asks for something that "follows logically from the statements" provided, which means the correct answer will be an Inference that must be true.

Step 2: Untangle the Stimulus

The stimulus provides two pieces of Formal Logic: If the standards committee has a quorum, the general assembly will begin at 6 PM. If the awards committee has a quorum, the general assembly will begin at 7 PM.

If	standards committee quorum	→	*6 PM start time*

If	awards committee quorum	→	*7 PM start time*

Step 3: Make a Prediction

The time of the assembly is set if either committee reaches its quorum. However, each committee reaching a quorum would result in a different start time for the assembly. So, only one committee could possibly get a quorum. It should also be noted that it's possible neither quorum will be met. In that case, there is no restriction on time. The assembly could still begin at 6 PM or 7 PM, or maybe any other time (e.g., 8:51 PM). In short, there are three possible outcomes: 1) Standards committee has a quorum, and the assembly is at 6 PM. 2) Awards committee has a quorum, and the assembly is at 7 PM. 3) Neither committee has a quorum, and the assembly can be scheduled at any time.

Step 4: Evaluate the Answer Choices

(E) must be true. If the standards committee has a quorum, the assembly will start at 6 PM, not 7 PM, and thus it's impossible for the awards committee to also have a quorum.

(A) could be false. If the assembly does not begin at 6 PM, then, by contrapositive, it must be true the standards committee doesn't have a quorum. However, that doesn't mean the awards committee does. It's possible neither committee has a quorum.

(B) could be false. There's no guarantee that either committee has a quorum. It's possible that both committees fail to meet a quorum.

(C) gets the Formal Logic backwards. The standards committee having a quorum is sufficient to guarantee a 6 PM start time. However, it's not necessary. The assembly could still begin at 6 PM even if the standards committee does not have a quorum (as long as the awards committee also does not have a quorum).

(D) is incorrect due to the same logic as **(A)**. If the assembly does not begin at 7 PM, then, by contrapositive, it must be true the awards committee doesn't have a quorum. However, that doesn't mean the standards committee does. It's possible neither committee has a quorum.

19. (A) Paradox

Step 1: Identify the Question Type

The question asks for something that will "resolve the apparent discrepancy," making this a Paradox question.

Step 2: Untangle the Stimulus

Lenders want to make sure potential borrowers don't default on a loan (i.e., fail to pay it back), so they usually look at borrowers' credit scores, as higher credit scores usually indicate lower risk of default. *Yet*, the inverse seems to happen with mortgage loans. For mortgage loans, default rates are *higher* for people with high credit scores.

Step 3: Make a Prediction

As with any Paradox question, take a moment to paraphrase the mystery. Why do people with high credit scores default on mortgage loans so frequently if high credit scores usually indicate a low risk of default? There must be something different about a mortgage loan that makes people with high credit scores more likely to default. Don't bother predicting an exact resolution. Instead, look for an answer that shows something particular about mortgage loans that would affect people with high credit scores.

Step 4: Evaluate the Answer Choices

(A) is correct. Other lenders consider a variety of risk factors. So, they might be more likely to deny a person with a high credit score because of other factors that increase the risk of default. Mortgage lenders don't consider the other factors for those with high credit scores, so those lenders are more likely to approve people with higher risks of default (despite the high credit score), and that would explain the discrepancy.

(B) does not help. Even if these credit scores *sometimes* have errors, that's not enough to suggest those errors are frequent enough or significant enough to cause such a discrepancy. Furthermore, it still doesn't explain why the defaults are much higher for those with the *highest* credit scores.

(C) is Out of Scope. It doesn't matter how the credit score is calculated. This offers no explanation why mortgage lenders see a greater rate of default for those with the highest credit scores.

(D) does not help. Even if borrowers were more likely to default on large loans (e.g., a mortgage), the mystery would still remain why those with the highest credit scores defaulted at a higher rate than those with lower credit scores.

(E) is irrelevant. The mystery is only about those people with the highest credits scores. Even if most people don't have such high scores, that has no effect on explaining what happens to the people who *do* have those high scores.

20. (D) Principle (Identify/Strengthen)

Step 1: Identify the Question Type

The question directly asks for a principle, and one that would "justify the reasoning" given, making this an Identify the Principle question that works like a Strengthen question.

Step 2: Untangle the Stimulus

The author concludes ([s]*o*) that people understand their mind's analytical capabilities more than they do their senses. The evidence is that creating computer models to perform reasoning (e.g., play chess) is easier than creating computer models to process senses (e.g., see things).

Step 3: Make a Prediction

The argument makes a dramatic Scope shift. The evidence is about our relative ease in creating certain computer models. The conclusion is about what we understand about ourselves. The author assumes these ideas are related; i.e., the easier it is to model some ability by computer, the better we understand that ability. The correct answer will verify this assumption in a broad manner.

Step 4: Evaluate the Answer Choices

(D) is correct. This matches the author's logic about how it's easier for us to model reasoning on a computer than it is to model senses, and thus we better understand reasoning (analytical capabilities) than we do our senses.

(A) is a Distortion. The author does not relate computer modeling to our actual *performance* of certain abilities. The author relates computer modeling to our *understanding* of those abilities.

(B) is a Distortion. The comparison involves how easy it is for us to create computer models, not how well we understand the computer's ability to perform those tasks.

(C) is Out of Scope. Intelligence has no role in this argument.

(E) is Out of Scope. There is no discussion or indication of how useful computer modeling is.

21. (B) Assumption (Necessary)

Step 1: Identify the Question Type

The question asks for an assumption on which the argument *depends*, making this a Necessary Assumption question.

Step 2: Untangle the Stimulus

The archaeologist concludes (*therefore*) that Canadian Aboriginals built birchbark canoes about 5,000 years ago. The evidence is that 5,000-year-old tools were discovered in the region, and Aboriginals recently used similar tools to make birchbark canoes.

Step 3: Make a Prediction

The tools may be 5,000 years old, but were they actually *used* at that time by Canadian Aboriginals to make the canoes? The archaeologist must assume that, if the tools date back 5,000 years, then they were used by Canadian Aboriginals at that time.

Step 4: Evaluate the Answer Choices

(B) must be assumed. The Canadian Aboriginals would need to have had those tools to use them. If, by the Denial Test, the tools were *not* present in the area back then, then they were likely used by some other group of people elsewhere. The Canadian Aboriginals would have acquired the tools later, and thus there would be no evidence that they were able to build the canoes 5,000 years ago.

(A) is Out of Scope. The trade value is irrelevant. Even if Aboriginals traded some of their tools away, they could have still saved some to make the birchbark canoes, as the archaeologist suggests.

(C) is Extreme. The archaeologist doesn't argue that the tools were *only* used on this material. Even if the tools had other uses, they still could have been used to build canoes.

(D) is Extreme. The archaeologist is not arguing that these tools were the *only* ones that could have been used. Even if there were other tools available, the argument still stands: Canoes could have been built 5,000 years ago.

(E) is Extreme. The archaeologist doesn't claim the tools couldn't be used for other tasks. They could have been used for dozens of tasks, and the archaeologist could still claim they were also used to make canoes. This may remove a potential weakener, but it is not necessary.

22. (A) Flaw

Step 1: Identify the Question Type
The question asks why the argument is "vulnerable to criticism," a commonly used phrase to indicate the argument has a flaw.

Step 2: Untangle the Stimulus
The advertisement is claiming that a particular hypnosis video is extremely effective. To effectively change one's behavior, directions must be given repeatedly to one's subconscious. The video does this by putting viewers into a hypnotic state. At that point, the viewer's subconscious is given a command to experience every instruction as if it were repeated 1,000 times. So, whenever the viewer hears a new command, the subconscious now experiences it 1,000 times, creating the repetition needed for success.

Step 3: Make a Prediction
There's just one catch. Okay, there are probably a lot of catches. However, stick to the logical error: For a command to be effective, it needs to be repeated frequently. Yet, the video gives a single initial command just once to the subconscious (experience all future commands 1,000 times), and it's expected that the subconscious will obey that command without repetition. That completely contradicts the evidence that commands have to be repeated many times to be effective. If the initial command isn't repeated many times, then the subconscious won't obey it and thus won't experience future commands any differently. Hence, the video becomes ineffective. The advertisement conveniently overlooks that loophole.

Step 4: Evaluate the Answer Choices
(A) is correct. By expecting the initial command to work immediately, the advertisement ignores its own claim that commands need to be repeated many times in order to be effective.

(B) is Extreme. The effectiveness does not *always* have to be *directly* proportional to the number of repetitions. Even if there's a limit to the effectiveness (e.g., directions are no more effective after the 600th time), the 1,000 repetitions can be more than enough to create the desired results.

(C) is Extreme. The advertisement merely claims that the video is "extremely effective," not the *most* effective technique.

(D) is not accurate. Only the conclusion claims the product is effective. The evidence is completely separate. There is no repeated claim.

(E) is a commonly tested flaw, but is not being tested here. This flaw is exemplified by people who claim unicorns are real because there's no evidence that they're fake. However, the advertisement makes no mention of people failing to prove that the hypnosis video is ineffective.

23. (C) Strengthen

Step 1: Identify the Question Type
The question asks for something that "adds the most support" to the given argument. That means it will Strengthen the argument.

Step 2: Untangle the Stimulus
The question asks about the historians' argument, which challenges the traditional view of Caligula as a cruel and insane tyrant. So, simply put, the historians argue that Caligula was not cruel and insane. As evidence, they cite a lack of documentation regarding such behavior. Further, whatever documents do exist were written by Caligula's enemies.

Step 3: Make a Prediction
There may not be a lot of evidence against Caligula, but it does still exist. The historians assume that the small volume of evidence and the questionable source of such attacks are enough to dismiss the content itself. However, if the behavior described is accurate and Caligula did commit some heinous acts, then the historians don't have much of an argument. To support the historians' claims, it would help to further question the accuracy and/or the credibility of what little evidence is left.

Step 4: Evaluate the Answer Choices
(C) is correct. If this is true, then it appears that the few stories that survived aren't even about Caligula. They're just stories about what other terrible people did and were repeated to suggest Caligula did them. That kind of deception would help the historians argue that Caligula has been misrepresented.

(A) is an Irrelevant Comparison. It doesn't matter how the quantity of documents from Caligula's time compares to that of other times. If the relatively few documents are still accurate, the historians' argument is invalid.

(B) is a 180, at worst. If people living under tyrants are unhappy, then the writings of such people would likely express such unhappiness. And if the surviving documents about Caligula express this unhappiness at his behavior, then it's possible he was a tyrant after all.

(D) is a 180. This suggests that Caligula has been described as even worse than other supposed tyrants, which doesn't bode well for the historians' attempted defense.

(E) is an Irrelevant Comparison. Even if some modern-day people commit even worse acts than Caligula, that doesn't help clear Caligula's name. He could still have been a cruel tyrant, even if he wasn't the worst of all time.

24. (B) Assumption (Sufficient)

Step 1: Identify the Question Type
The question asks for something that logically completes the argument. Fill-in-the-blank questions are usually Inference questions, but this is an exception. The blank is preceded by the word *because*, which indicates evidence. So, the blank will be filled in with an unstated piece of evidence that will logically complete the argument, i.e., a sufficient assumption.

Step 2: Untangle the Stimulus
Critics are arguing that a plan for creating new building sites will reduce the habitat area for local dolphins. The author claims they are mistaken, essentially arguing that the plan will not reduce the dolphin's habitat. The evidence is...well...there is no evidence. It's said that dolphins don't swim in deep water (greater than 30 meters deep), but the plan intends to use land that is under just 5 meters of water.

Step 3: Make a Prediction
If the dolphins swim in the area being taken over for new building sites, then their habitat size will be reduced. In order to conclude otherwise, the author has to assume one of two things: 1) When the land is taken over, additional areas in that habitat will open up to dolphins to make up for the lost area, or 2) the land being taken over is not actually part of the dolphin's habitat, so the dolphins won't actually be losing anything. The correct answer will confirm one of these assumptions.

Step 4: Evaluate the Answer Choices
(B) is correct. The land being taken over as part of the plan is only 5 meters deep. If dolphins don't inhabit areas that shallow, then taking over that land will have no effect on the dolphins' habitat, exactly as the author suggests.

(A) is Out of Scope. The argument is not about maintaining the population size of the dolphins. It's solely about the size of their habitat area. Even if the remaining area is still plenty large enough to support the dolphin population, taking away

any area will still reduce the habitat size, contrary to the author's argument.

(C) is Out of Scope. The argument is solely about the size of the habitat area, not what is most threatening to the dolphins. Even if there are bigger threats, taking away areas will still reduce the dolphins' habitat, contrary to the author's claim.

(D) is irrelevant. The average depth does not affect what's going to happen. Once the intended land is taken away, the size of the habitat will still be smaller, contrary to the author's claim. Dolphins may prefer the slightly deeper water of 25 meters, but if they are able to use the 5-meter-deep water as a habitat, then the building plan would still reduce their available habitat.

(E) is irrelevant, and a 180 at worst. The dolphins won't swim in that area where the depth is 100 meters. And when the intended land is taken over, there will be even less room for the dolphins before the ocean floor drops. So, this does not prove the critics are mistaken, but instead merely indicates the dolphins' habitat is already closely bound on one side.

25. (C) Parallel Reasoning

Step 1: Identify the Question Type
The correct answer will be an argument with reasoning that is "similar to that" in the author's argument. That makes this a Parallel Reasoning question.

Step 2: Untangle the Stimulus
The author presents a piece of Formal Logic: Any popular TV show that is groundbreaking is critically acclaimed. However, not all popular TV shows are critically acclaimed. Thus, the author concludes they're not all groundbreaking.

Step 3: Make a Prediction
The logic here is solid, but use a quick translation to see why. According to the opening claim, if a popular show is groundbreaking, then it's also critically acclaimed. By contrapositive, that means if a popular show is not critically acclaimed, then it is not groundbreaking.

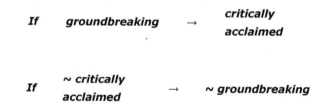

If *not all* popular shows are critically acclaimed, that means some of them are *not* critically acclaimed. By contrapositive, that means they're not groundbreaking, confirming the conclusion that not all popular shows are groundbreaking (i.e., some are not). The correct answer will utilize a contrapositive in the exact same way: All members of a group (popular shows) that are X (groundbreaking) are Y (critically acclaimed), so if some members of that group are *not* Y, then some members cannot be X.

Step 4: Evaluate the Answer Choices

(C) is a match. All members of a group (biographies) that are X (unbiased) are Y (have embarrassing facts). Because some members of that group are not Y (not all biographies have embarrassing facts, i.e., some don't), the author logically concludes, by contrapositive, that some members are not X (not all biographies are unbiased, i.e., some aren't).

If	**unbiased**	→	**embarrassing facts**
If	**~ embarrassing facts**	→	**~ unbiased**

(A) does not match. This takes a general claim about one group of items (articles), but moves to another general claim about *all* members of a different group of items (academic works). And unlike the original argument, the conclusion here contains an If/Then statement.

(B) does not match. This gets the Formal Logic backwards. Here, the original logic is: If a student's work is greatly improved, then the student gets high grades. However, the rest of the logic is about students who *do* get high grades, as opposed to ones who *don't*. There's no using the contrapositive. Also, this is illogical. The students who get high grades may get those high grades for other reasons.

(D) does not match. This does have a piece of Formal Logic (if someone is polite to Schwartz, then he is polite in return). However, the rest of the argument applies that logic to *all* members of a specific subgroup (his colleagues) as opposed to just some people. Additionally, it does not utilize the contrapositive of the logic.

(E) does not match. This does have a piece of Formal Logic about members of a group (books), and it does apply that logic to *some* items in that group. However, the applied logic is not proper. The initial Formal Logic is this:

If	**worth reading**	→	**worth buying**

The next claim is that there are some books that are *not* worth reading. However, that doesn't mean they're not worth buying. That negates the logic without reversing it. It's not the proper contrapositive. The books can still be worth buying for other reasons. If the second sentence of **(E)** had said, "So, since not all books are worth *buying*, not all books are worth *reading*," then it would have been parallel.

Section II: Reading Comprehension

Passage 1: Chinatown Chinese

Q#	Question Type	Correct	Difficulty
1	Global	C	★
2	Inference	C	★
3	Logic Function	E	★
4	Detail	A	★
5	Inference	A	★★★

Passage 2: The Improbable Nature of the Universe

Q#	Question Type	Correct	Difficulty
6	Global	A	★★
7	Inference	B	★
8	Inference	D	★
9	Inference	D	★
10	Logic Function	C	★★
11	Inference	C	★★
12	Logic Reasoning (Parallel Reasoning)	B	★

Passage 3: Social Norms as a Substitute for Legal Protection

Q#	Question Type	Correct	Difficulty
13	Global	E	★
14	Detail	C	★★
15	Detail	B	★
16	Inference	B	★
17	Inference	E	★★
18	Logic Reasoning (Parallel Reasoning)	D	★★
19	Inference	A	★★★★
20	Logic Reasoning (Strengthen)	B	★★

Passage 4: Charlotte Perkins Gilman and Social Darwinism

Q#	Question Type	Correct	Difficulty
21	Global	D	★★
22	Inference	E	★★★★
23	Global	A	★★
24	Detail	D	★★
25	Detail	B	★★★
26	Global	B	★★★
27	Inference	A	★★★

Passage 1: Chinatown Chinese

Step 1: Read the Passage Strategically
Sample Roadmap

Line #	Keyword/phrase	¶ Margin notes
3	argues	**Linguists: Chinatown Chinese is new dialect**
7	based primarily; two claims; first	Evid -
7–8	so different	1) language is different
10	difficult time	
12	second	2) anyone can learn
14	effectively	
15	so long	
17	Regarding the first claim	Auth: problem with 1st claim
25	However	
27	But	Core of language is same
28	but not	
29	In fact	
37	supposed	
38	barrier; therefore; mostly imaginary	
39	second claim	Auth: problem with 2nd claim
43	misleading oversimplification; While	Too simplistic
49	not	Ex. Cantonese understood, not shared
50	Moreover	
50–51	differ markedly	dialects vary
53	differences persist	
54	Hence; even	
56–57	does not guarantee	Easy communication not guaranteed
57	because	
58	only a minute	

Discussion

The passage opens by noting how there are many dialects of the Chinese language, and some linguists argue that "Chinatown Chinese," a version of Chinese spoken in San Francisco's Chinatown, constitutes such a dialect. The linguists provide two claims to support this contention: 1) It's so different from other dialects that someone new to the U.S. from China would have trouble communicating with Chinese Americans in Chinatown. 2) If they learn the unique terms of Chinatown Chinese, people from China can communicate easily regardless of their traditional dialect. At this point, Chinatown Chinese serves as the **Topic** of the passage. The **Scope** revolves around the question of whether that language constitutes a unique dialect.

Over the next two paragraphs, the author rejects both of the linguist's claims, and this rejection serves as the **Purpose** of the passage. In the second paragraph, the author directly attacks the first claim of how different Chinatown Chinese is. The author argues that many of the unique terms are merely proper names or references to things not experienced in China (e.g., downtown or Labor Day). These can be easily explained and don't have to hinder conversation. The author claims, *therefore*, that the purported language barrier is "mostly imaginary."

In the third paragraph, the author attacks the second claim, calling it a "misleading oversimplification." For one thing, people have become familiar with other dialects (e.g., Cantonese), but that doesn't make it a shared dialect. Furthermore, different dialects can have very different sounds and grammar. There's no guarantee that people of any dialect can suddenly start communicating easily with Chinese Americans just by adding a few common terms such as city or street names. While not directly stated, the author's arguments in the last two paragraphs establish the **Main Idea** that the linguists' claims in support of Chinatown Chinese as a new dialect are not particularly persuasive. It's useful to note that the author never actually argues that Chinatown Chinese is *not* a distinct dialect. The author merely challenges the linguists' claims in support of that designation. Recognizing this can help efficiently evaluate some answer choices.

1. (C) Global

Step 2: Identify the Question Type
The question asks for the "main point of the passage," making this a Global question.

Step 3: Research the Relevant Text
There's no need to go back into the text of the passage. Instead, consider the Main Idea as determined while reading strategically.

Step 4: Make a Prediction
The author's main point was that the linguists' claims supporting Chinatown Chinese as a new dialect are not very persuasive.

Step 5: Evaluate the Answer Choices
(C) matches the author's purpose and main theme.

(A) is Half-Right, Half-Wrong. The author does argue that the linguists are mistaken, but not for this reason. And the author never even suggests that Chinatown Chinese is intelligible to those who speak Cantonese.

(B) is a 180, at worst. This focuses merely on a narrow and distorted interpretation of the linguists' claims in the first paragraph, which the author goes on to reject throughout the passage.

(D) is too narrow and a Distortion. This focuses too much on the second paragraph, in which the author argues that the language barrier is "mostly imaginary" (line 38). It ignores the reasoning in the third paragraph, which suggests that easy conversation is *not* guaranteed, despite some common vocabulary. Also, the author is not technically rejecting Chinatown Chinese as a dialect. The author is merely challenging the linguists' claims in support of that classification.

(E) is Extreme. The author questions the claims of some linguists. There's no indication of any consensus among linguists overall, let alone a reversal of the opinion about Chinatown Chinese as a new dialect.

2. (C) Inference

Step 2: Identify the Question Type
The question asks for something the "passage suggests," making this an Inference question.

Step 3: Research the Relevant Text
The question asks specifically about what a visitor from China would have difficulty discussing with a Chinese American. The linguists claim that difficulty arises because the language is "so different from any other dialect" (lines 7–8). The author provides specific examples in the second paragraph, and those will be useful for this question.

Step 4: Make a Prediction
According to lines 17–25, a lot of the distinctive vocabulary consists of geographical names (e.g., city names) and things that visitors "had never encountered in China." So, a visitor would find it hardest to talk about things unique to U.S. culture.

Step 5: Evaluate the Answer Choices
(C) is correct. A Chinese American's daily life is more likely to revolve around local settings with distinctly American details.

(A) is a Distortion. The difficulty is that visitors from China would be unfamiliar with U.S. concepts, not that Chinese Americans would be unfamiliar with events in China.

(B) is a 180. If the relatives are mutual, then this would be shared knowledge, not unique names that are unfamiliar to the Chinese visitors.

(D) is Out of Scope. Feelings may be universal, and there's no evidence that discussing them would require any uniquely American vocabulary.

(E) is a 180. The difficulties come from new vocabulary that arose to describe American things, not traditional Chinese ideas.

3. (E) Logic Function

Step 2: Identify the Question Type
The phrase "in order to" indicates the question is asking why the author mentions certain terms, making this a Logic Function question.

Step 3: Research the Relevant Text
The words in question are brought up in the second paragraph. Use the margin notes to focus on the purpose of the paragraph in general, rather than worrying about the details.

Step 4: Make a Prediction
The purpose of the second paragraph is to show how much of the new vocabulary in Chinatown Chinese consists merely of words for American places and ideas. The two words in question are merely examples of such words: American ideas that have been incorporated into the language.

Step 5: Evaluate the Answer Choices
(E) is correct.

(A) is Extreme. These American-inspired terms make up much of the unique vocabulary, but there's no suggestion that such terms *dominate* the language as a whole. In fact, this is contradicted by the last sentence of the passage, which suggests that such terms are "generally peripheral to the core vocabulary" (lines 57–59).

(B) is Out of Scope, and a 180 at worst. The author is discussing communication between Chinese Americans and visitors from China, not communication among Chinese Americans. And lines 29–33 claim that conversation is only easy if people speak the *same* traditional dialect, not different ones.

(C) is a Faulty Use of Detail. The discussion of these terms is in the first part of the second paragraph, where the author discusses words based on American ideas. The idea of native Chinese people understanding Chinese Americans easily isn't discussed until after the Keyword [*h*]*owever* (line 25). And even then, it's restricted to those who speak the "same traditional Chinese dialect" (lines 32–33). By the last

paragraph, the author is arguing counter to this point, that native Chinese are not guaranteed to understand Chinese Americans with ease.

(D) is a 180. The author never directly advocates for or soundly rejects Chinatown Chinese as a dialect. The author's goal throughout the second (and third) paragraph is to argue against specific claims in favor of Chinatown Chinese as a dialect.

4. (A) Detail

Step 2: Identify the Question Type
The question asks for something about traditional Chinese dialects that is true "[a]ccording to the passage," making this a Detail question.

Step 3: Research the Relevant Text
The dialects of Chinese immigrants are mentioned throughout the passage, including lines 25–29 in the second paragraph and lines 50–59 in the third paragraph. The author claims that "the core of the language brought to the U.S. by Chinese people has remained intact" (lines 25–27). This is further supported by claims about how such dialects have merely been "supplemented, not supplanted" (lines 27–28) and how they "persist among Chinese-American speakers" (line 53).

Step 4: Make a Prediction
The correct answer will express how, despite the addition of new vocabulary words for American terms, the original dialects have remain virtually unchanged.

Step 5: Evaluate the Answer Choices
(A) matches the text of the passage.

(B) is Out of Scope. There is no mention of traditional dialects merging with each other.

(C) is a 180. The author claims that such differences as sound and grammar "persist among Chinese-American speakers" (lines 52–54). They don't change.

(D) is Extreme. The author claims that speakers of Chinese dialects have become "familiar with Cantonese" (lines 44–45), but there is no indication of people *abandoning* their traditional dialect in favor of Cantonese.

(E) is a 180. The author claims that American English terms have merely "supplemented, not supplanted" (lines 27–28) traditional dialects.

5. (A) Inference

Step 2: Identify the Question Type
The question asks for something the author "most likely means," which will be inferred from the text of the passage, making this an Inference question.

Step 3: Research the Relevant Text

The question points to line 22, and the phrase "such as" immediately following the phrase "transliterated terms" indicates an example to clarify the meaning of that phrase. It also helps to contrast this with "direct translations" described in the next sentence.

Step 4: Make a Prediction

The author uses the word *dang-tang*, which means "downtown," as an example of a transliterated term. The word *dang-tang* basically borrows the same structure of the American word *downtown* (a two-syllable compound word with a rhyming pair of words beginning with *d* and *t*, respectively). This is used in contrast to a direct translation, such as *gong-ngihn ngiht*, which just takes the exact Chinese words for *labor* and *day* to create the American phrase "Labor Day." So, transliterated terms have no direct Chinese counterpart, but are words created to just sound like their original counterparts.

Step 5: Evaluate the Answer Choices

(A) is correct. Words like *dang-tang* just take the sounds and meaning of American language (in this instance, rhyming compound words that refer to a particular location) and incorporate them into Chinese.

(B) is a Distortion. While *downtown* is part of the local American experience, so are terms like "Labor Day," which are *not* translated into transliterated terms. Transliterated terms refer to a particular subset of words that are designed to sound like their American counterparts.

(C) is Out of Scope. The author does not discuss how these words are written.

(D) is a 180. Direct translations are distinct from transliterated terms. Direct translations are word-for-word translations of a term (e.g., the Chinese American translation of "Labor Day"), whereas transliterated terms attempt to mimic the sound of the term being translated (e.g., the Chinese-American translation of *downtown*).

(E) is a 180. The transliterated terms are meant to sound similar to their original counterparts and would expectedly sound similar from one dialect to the next.

Passage 2: The Improbable Nature of the Universe

Step 1: Read the Passage Strategically
Sample Roadmap

Line #	Keyword/phrase	¶ Margin notes
4	If	**Action hero - just avoids death**
5	Yet	
7	resembles	Universe = hero: small change = disaster
10	impossible	
11	For example	Ex. different forces = no life
14	Indeed	
15	must	Auth: life is improbable
16	so finely tuned	
17	improbable	
18	reconcile	
19–20	seeming improbability	
20	hypothesizing	Comsol explain multiverse
21	but one	
25	But	Ours is one of many; ours is just right
26	good chance	
28	But; how exceptional	Is our universe really special?
29	?	
30–31	arises largely from the difficulty	Scientists can't find alternative
		Scientists tweak one element to test
38	But	
39	no reason	Auth: tweak multiple elements and find many alternatives
42–43	very different	
43	yet compatible	
48	therefore	
48–49	call... into question?	
49	I do not this is necessarily the case	Auth: multiverse is still possible
50	two reasons; First	
52	Secondly	

Discussion

In the first paragraph, the author describes the incredible fortune that befalls action movie heroes. They survive countless experiences that, if things happened even slightly differently, could have resulted in certain death. And just as you start thinking, "Action movies? This is going to be the best LSAT passage ever," the author shifts dramatically in the second paragraph and proclaims, "Gotcha! That was just an analogy. We're really going to be talking about the universe and physics!" And so, the universe is the **Topic** of the passage, not action movies.

As with the action hero, life in our universe has survived countless experiences that, if something had happened even a little bit differently, could have resulted in disaster. As an example, the author notes how slightly different nuclear forces would have denied the presence of carbon, which is needed for life. The idea that our universe just happened to get everything right seems to be improbable. So, how did our universe work out so perfectly? It's this question that serves as the **Scope** of the passage, and the **Purpose** is to provide some answers.

In the third paragraph, some cosmologists offer a suggestion: Our universe is not the only one. There's actually a multiverse that's filled with a wide array of different universes with different laws of physics. By the rules of probability, there was bound to be at least one (e.g., ours) that got the physics just right.

However, in the fourth paragraph, the author raises the question: Are our universe's laws of physics really that exceptional? Scientists seem to think so because they struggle to find viable alternative laws. As described in the fifth paragraph, they run simulations to test how things would be different if one physical aspect of the universe changed—and disaster ensues. *But*, the author takes a different approach: Why change just one parameter at a time? Along with a colleague, the author has tested scenarios with multiple changes and discovered many ways that life could form under very different sets of physical laws. It would appear our universe isn't so exceptional after all. And this serves as the **Main Idea** of the passage: Our universe might appear to be a unique version that somehow got everything just right, but life still could have survived under other scenarios, too.

The last paragraph raises one final question: If the author's findings are valid and life could have formed under various other scenarios, does that negate the multiverse theory? The author says no for two reasons: 1) The existence of a multiverse still seems plausible based on models of the universe, and 2) the concept of a multiverse can help solve other cosmological mysteries. This doesn't change the author's Main Idea, but it does show how the author is open-minded, which can be valuable when answering the questions.

6. (A) Global

Step 2: Identify the Question Type
The question asks for the "main point of the passage," making this a Global question.

Step 3: Research the Relevant Text
There's no need to go back into the passage. Instead, use the Main Idea determined from reading the passage strategically.

Step 4: Make a Prediction
The author's Main Idea is that our universe might appear to be the one that got the physics just right, but life could have survived with other combinations of physical laws, too.

Step 5: Evaluate the Answer Choices
(A) is correct.

(B) is too narrow. It focuses entirely on the last sentence of the passage with no reference to a major component of the passage: the author's discussion and research about other sets of physical laws that could support life.

(C) is too narrow, focusing only on a minor point made in the third paragraph. By the fourth paragraph, the author points out a flaw in the scientists' methodology to reveal the main point of the passage: that there are alternative sets of laws.

(D) is a Distortion. The theory of a multiverse is meant to explain the improbability of life, not the other way around. Besides, this ignores the major factor about the potential of other sets of physical laws that could result in life.

(E) is too narrow, focusing solely on the analogy described in the first two paragraphs. After the analogy is made, the author shifts the focus to how this has happened, despite the improbability.

7. (B) Inference

Step 2: Identify the Question Type
The question asks for something "inferred from the passage," making this an Inference question.

Step 3: Research the Relevant Text
The question asks about the meaning of a direct quote from the passage, and it even gives an exact location. Use the context around that quote to determine the meaning. The word *then* immediately before "play the movie" indicates this is a step in a process. In the previous sentence, the scientists start by tweaking a law of physics. It's then that they "play the movie," which the author details by providing a list of actions set off between dashes.

Step 4: Make a Prediction
This stage involves doing calculations, creating what-if scenarios, and running simulations. So, when scientists "play

the movie," they are testing what would happen if they tweaked a law of physics.

Step 5: Evaluate the Answer Choices

(B) matches this process. They take a theoretical event (changing a law of physics) and study the potential chain of events (running simulations to test what would happen).

(A) is a Distortion. While the scenarios being tested are hypothetical (and thus potentially fictional), the act being described ("play the movie") is an actual process that involves running calculations and simulations. That process is certainly not fictional.

(C) is a Distortion. The author might be using an analogy to make it sound dramatic, but there's no indication that the scientists use this term for dramatic purposes.

(D) is Out of Scope. There's no mention of any archetypes being used as a model.

(E) is a Distortion. If the *story* being told is that of the universe unfolding, then yes, the scientists do "shape the story" by tweaking the laws of physics. However, that's done before they "play the movie," which is more like watching what happens after their changes are made. It doesn't refer to the actual shaping of the story.

8. (D) Inference

Step 2: Identify the Question Type

The question asks for something the passage *suggests*, and something with which the cosmologists mentioned are "most likely to agree." That makes this an Inference question.

Step 3: Research the Relevant Text

The question stem directly references the third paragraph. The margin notes for that paragraph would be a good place to start.

Step 4: Make a Prediction

The third paragraph presents the cosmologists' hypothesis that there are multiple universes, and ours just happened to get the physics exactly right to support life. The correct answer will be consistent with this.

Step 5: Evaluate the Answer Choices

(D) is a match, mimicking the idea that "the sheer number of possibilities" provided "a good chance" to get it right "at least once" (lines 25–27).

(A) is Out of Scope. There is no mention of how any one universe affects the others, let alone ours.

(B) is a 180. The existence of multiple universes makes it more likely that at least one contains life. However, it's still claimed that "almost all" universes will still be incapable of supporting life.

(C) is a 180. The whole idea of a multiverse is that each universe has its own laws of physics, and our universe is one with the "right" set of laws.

(E) is Extreme. The cosmologists say there's a good chance to get the right set of laws "at least once" (line 27), not *only* once.

9. (D) Inference

Step 2: Identify the Question Type

The question asks for something with which the author is "most likely to agree," making this an Inference question.

Step 3: Research the Relevant Text

The conventional investigation method of scientists, as well as the author's reaction, is found in the fifth paragraph.

Step 4: Make a Prediction

The conventional method is to take a particular physical law, tweak it, and test what happens. *But*, the author argues "there is no reason to tweak just one parameter at a time" (lines 38–39). The author then describes successful experiments in which multiple parameters are tweaked. So, the author finds the scientists to be restrictive in testing just one parameter at a time.

Step 5: Evaluate the Answer Choices

(D) is correct. The scientists only test results of changing one constant, when they could be more open and test the changing of multiple constants.

(A) is a 180. The results are certainly relevant. The scientists are just too limited in what they test.

(B) is a 180, at worst. If anything, the scientists are *too* focused on testing one parameter at a time. They need to broaden their focus.

(C) is Out of Scope. The author is questioning what the scientists choose to study, not the effort (or rigor) they put into studying it.

(E) is a 180, at worst. The author claims that workable models are found when changing multiple parameters, not just one (as the scientists do). While the author may never explicitly deny the possibility of the scientists ever finding a model, there's no indication that they eventually will, either.

10. (C) Logic Function

Step 2: Identify the Question Type

The question asks how the final paragraph "functions primarily" within the passage, making this a Logic Function question.

Step 3: Research the Relevant Text

The margin notes for the final paragraph should be sufficient for determining the function.

Step 4: Make a Prediction
The last paragraph poses a question: Does the author's research deny the possibility of a multiverse? And the author argues that it really doesn't. So, the purpose of the paragraph is to determine what effect (in this case, not much) the author's research might have on the multiverse theory.

Step 5: Evaluate the Answer Choices
(C) is correct, as the paragraph questions the effects, or implications, of the author's research.

(A) is a Distortion. The final paragraph focuses on the multiverse theory, which the author does not say is inadequate. On the contrary, the author argues the multiverse theory may still be valid. The author only argues against the scientists' methods, but that happens in the previous paragraph.

(B) is a Distortion. The author does say that the multiverse theory may answer other cosmological questions, but that's the multiverse theory, not the author's research. Besides, there's no indication of what kinds of questions that theory could address.

(D) is a Distortion and a 180, at worst. The two points in the final paragraph discuss how the author's position affects the multiverse theory, not how anything affects the author's position. Furthermore, the author claims there is no contradiction, so there are no counterarguments.

(E) is a Distortion. The paragraph is about the effect of the author's research on the multiverse theory, not how to continue the author's research.

11. (C) Inference

Step 2: Identify the Question Type
The question asks for the "author's attitude," which is a common variant of Inference questions. The author's attitude won't be stated, but it will be supported by the author's use of language.

Step 3: Research the Relevant Text
The multiverse is first mentioned in the third paragraph, but that's primarily the cosmologists' point of view. The author's opinions are more openly displayed in the final paragraph.

Step 4: Make a Prediction
In the final paragraph, the author directly asks whether research calls the multiverse theory into question. And the author's answer: "I do not think [so]." The author goes on to say how certain models still support it and that it "may well prove to be" useful. So, the author at least acknowledges it as plausible, even if the language isn't forceful enough to suggest absolute belief.

Step 5: Evaluate the Answer Choices
(C) matches the author's tone. The author accepts the possibility that the multiverse theory *may* still be useful.

(A) is a 180. The author argues that some universal models support the existence of the multiverse and that it may well prove to be useful.

(B) is a 180. The author argues that certain models make it likely the multiverse *does* exist.

(D) is Extreme. The author claims that research doesn't deny the possibility of a multiverse, but the author doesn't outright advocate for the multiverse theory, either. The author only acknowledges that it *may* be useful.

(E) is Extreme. The author only indicates that the multiverse theory is not negated by research and that it *may* be useful. That kind of language does not indicate enthusiasm.

12. (B) Logic Reasoning (Parallel Reasoning)

Step 2: Identify the Question Type
The question asks for something that would make one situation *analogous* to another. That's a term that indicates Parallel Reasoning, a question type typically found in Logical Reasoning.

Step 3: Research the Relevant Text
The question refers to the both the first and third paragraphs. The correct answer will add logic to the first paragraph to make it more parallel to the logic of the situation in the third paragraph.

Step 4: Make a Prediction
The movie hero in the first paragraph is said to survive despite incredible odds. This was said to be parallel to our universe, which has also survived despite incredible odds. The multiverse theory in the third paragraph says that our universe has survived because it is one of many universes, and happens to be one that just managed to get everything right. So, to be consistent with that logic, the hero from the action movie would be one of many possible heroes, but one who just happens to get everything right and avoid certain death.

Step 5: Evaluate the Answer Choices
(B) is logically parallel, making the hero one of many possible heroes, but one who beats the odds while almost all others do not.

(A) does not match. This would be similar to our universe getting support from other universes, which is not what happens in the multiverse theory.

(C) does not match. The multiverse theory is about multiple universes, not the same universe adapting through a series of events.

(D) is Extreme and does not match. In the multiverse theory, almost all other universes fail to support life (lines 22–25). They don't all succeed.

(E) is Out of Scope and does not match. This has no relation to our universe, which was not given any kind of *map* on how to avoid disaster and support life.

Passage 3: Social Norms as a Substitute for Legal Protection

Step 1: Read the Passage Strategically
Sample Roadmap

Line #	Keyword/phrase	¶ Margin notes
Passage A		
2	might expect	**Joke-stealing**
5	Yet	
6–7	all but unheard of	No legal action
7	despite	
9	product of both	1) Too expensive
		2) Hard to win
13	In the end	
14	simply does not	
16	holds	
18	scant	Lack of legal protection should deter creativity
19	deterred; unlikelihood	
20	If	
20-21	no effective	
21	why	Why not?
23	?	
24	The answer	
25	substitute for	Comedians use social norms
28–29	not merely	
32	serious; harm	Violators shunned
33	substantially hamper	
Passage B		
40	very valuable	
41	not	Recipes lack legal protection
42	effectively covered	
45	but	
46	seldom; Instead; three	Chefs use social norms instead
48	quite similar	
50	First	1) Don't copy
56	second	2) Don't share
61	third	3) Give credit

Discussion

Passage A begins by discussing comedians, who don't like other people stealing their jokes. They could protect their jokes with copyright laws, but they rarely do, despite how frequently jokes get stolen. The author offers two reasons for the lack of lawsuits: 1) They're expensive, and 2) they're difficult to win.

In the second paragraph, the author raises an interesting question. Why do comedians continue to create new material despite the potential risks? The third paragraph offers an answer. Comedians protect themselves using social norms as a substitute for actual laws. If one comedian tries to steal jokes, the other comedians take actions (e.g., badmouthing) that could ruin the joke stealer's reputation and potentially that person's career.

So, the **Topic** of passage A is comedians, and the **Scope** is how they protect their material through social norms. The **Purpose** is merely to inform the reader. The **Main Idea** is that, because copyright laws are expensive and difficult to enforce against joke stealing, comedians use social norms as a way to protect their creative material.

Passage B shifts the **Topic** to a new group of professionals: chefs. In this case, chefs want to protect their recipes. Recipes are generally not protected by intellectual property, patent, or copyright laws, but they could potentially be protected by trade secrecy laws. However, like the comedians, chefs rarely take legal action. Instead, also like comedians, chefs opt to protect themselves with social norms.

The second paragraph details the three social norms by which chefs operate. First, chefs cannot copy another chef's recipe exactly, effectively treating the recipe like a patent. Second, if a chef shares the recipe with a colleague, the colleague cannot share it with anyone else. This effectively creates something akin to a trade secrecy contract. Third, colleagues must give credit to the person who actually developed the recipe, which creates a sort of copyright protection.

While passage B has a completely different Topic, it essentially shares everything else. The **Scope** is how chefs protect their recipes through social norms. The **Purpose** is to inform the reader. The **Main Idea** is that chefs rarely take legal action to protect their recipes and instead rely on social norms for protection.

So, the passages have a lot in common. And besides the difference in Topic, there are a few other key differences that are worth noting. Unlike passage B, passage A mentions why people don't take legal action (lines 8–15) and outlines specific consequences of violating the rules of social norms (lines 29–34). And unlike passage A, passage B relates social norms to numerous legal counterparts, such as patents (lines

51–55), trade secrecy (lines 59–61), and copyright (lines 63–64).

13. (E) Global

Step 2: Identify the Question Type
The question asks for something about which both passages are "primarily concerned," making this a Global question.

Step 3: Research the Relevant Text
There's no need to go back into the text. Use the Topic and Scope, as determined while reading the passages.

Step 4: Make a Prediction
Both passages focus on describing how a group of professionals (comedians in passage A and chefs in passage B) choose to use social norms instead of legal recourse to protect their creative works (jokes and recipes, respectively).

Step 5: Evaluate the Answer Choices
(E) is correct.

(A) is a Faulty Use of Detail. Both passages do mention legal protections briefly at the beginning, but the primary focus in both passages is about how the groups in question eschew legal protection and instead use social norms for protection.

(B) is Out of Scope for passage B, which never mentions any incentives for creating new material. Only passage A makes a connection to incentives in lines 34–38.

(C) is Out of Scope. Neither passage discusses the social value of making their creations publicly available.

(D) is Out of Scope for passage B, which never discusses why chefs don't take legal action. Only passage A does that in lines 8–15.

14. (C) Detail

Step 2: Identify the Question Type
The question asks for something directly discussed in the passage, making this a Detail question.

Step 3: Research the Relevant Text
Instead of reading through all of the text again, consider the relationship between the passages and what key differences are present.

Step 4: Make a Prediction
As predicted after reading the passage, there are two major ideas covered in passage A that are not covered in passage B: 1) the reasons why comedians don't take legal action (lines 8–15) and 2) the specific consequences for people who break social norms (lines 29–34).

Step 5: Evaluate the Answer Choices
(C) is correct. Passage A mentions enforcement via badmouthing and refusing to work with joke stealers (lines 29–34). Passage B only mentions the rules with no mention of how they are enforced.

(A) is a 180. Passage B does compare social norms to intellectual property laws throughout the passage (lines 40–44, lines 46–49, etc.).

(B) is Out of Scope. Neither passage discusses how social norms evolved.

(D) is Out of Scope. Neither passage mentions how social norms may be limited.

(E) is Out of Scope. Neither passage discusses how social norms impact creative output. They only discuss how social norms are used to protect the material that is created.

15. (B) Detail

Step 2: Identify the Question Type
The correct answer will be a question that is directly answered by details in the passage, making this a Detail question.

Step 3: Research the Relevant Text
The correct answer will refer to details in passage A that are not mentioned in passage B. Instead of going through all of the text, start by considering the relationship between the passages and the key differences.

Step 4: Make a Prediction
Unlike passage B, passage A discusses why comedians don't take legal action (lines 8–15) and how they enforce the rules upon those who break them (lines 29–34). The correct answer will likely raise a question about one of these differences.

Step 5: Evaluate the Answer Choices
(B) is correct. Only passage A explains why legal action is avoided: It's expensive and difficult to win (lines 8–15). Passage B only states that chefs rarely take legal action (lines 44–46), but never offers any reason why.

(A) is a 180. Passage A never talks about sharing creative work. In fact, only passage B mentions that in lines 56–64.

(C) is a 180. Only passage B, not passage A, ever brings up the idea of patents (line 43).

(D) is a 180. Passage B explicitly mentions recipes as a form of creative output regarded as intellectual property (lines 39–40).

(E) is a 180. The entire second paragraph of passage B describes specific social norms that prohibit the violation of intellectual property rights.

16. (B) Inference

Step 2: Identify the Question Type
The question asks for something with which the author of passage A is "most likely to agree," making this an Inference question.

Step 3: Research the Relevant Text
The question does not refer to any specific idea in passage A, so the entire text is relevant.

Step 4: Make a Prediction
An exact prediction here is unlikely, if not impossible. Instead, go through the answers individually. Eliminate anything that is not consistent with the big picture, and use content clues in the choices to do any research, as necessary.

Step 5: Evaluate the Answer Choices
(B) is correct. The author mentions that comedians don't pursue legal action in part because success in such lawsuits is "difficult and uncertain" (line 12). So, if it weren't so difficult and uncertain (i.e., success were more assured), comedians would be more willing to consider it.

(A) is Out of Scope. The author of passage A never mentions or discusses how comedians influence one another.

(C) is Out of Scope for passage A. Only passage B mentions trade secrecy law. There is no indication that the author of passage A has any opinion about how trade secrecy would apply to jokes.

(D) is a 180. In the last sentence (lines 34–38), the author mentions how comedians are able to assert ownership of their jokes, effectively enforcing rules and maintaining the incentive to create more. There is no indication the author finds social norms ineffective at any level.

(E) is a 180. The whole point of the third paragraph is to describe how comedians have developed an informal system that can be just as effective as formal legal protection.

17. (E) Inference

Step 2: Identify the Question Type
The question asks for something that is "most strongly supported" by the passages. That makes this an Inference question.

Step 3: Research the Relevant Text
There are no specific references or content clues, making the entire text relevant.

Step 4: Make a Prediction
Because the correct answer can be based on anything in either passage (or both), it will be nearly impossible to make an exact prediction. Instead, test the choices individually using the big picture of both passages as a guideline.

Step 5: Evaluate the Answer Choices
(E) is correct. Passage A mentions how the system of social norms allows comedians to assert ownership of jokes and maintain incentives to create new material (lines 34–38), and passage B mentions how social norms provide chefs with protection similar to that gained under legal intellectual property systems (lines 46–49).

(A) is Out of Scope. The authors never address one another, and neither makes any comparison between comedians and chefs.

(B) is not supported. Passage A does not describe the details of the norms system among comedians, only referring to it as governing "a wide array of issues" (line 27). There's no way to determine whether that system is more or less elaborate than the one described in passage B.

(C) is not supported. Passage A mentions that comedians can be protected by copyright laws and chefs can be protected by trade secrecy laws. But there's no indication that the appropriate legal protection is more significant for one group than for the other.

(D) is a 180, at worst. The fact that both groups rely on social norms instead of legal protection makes it seem that they are *not* satisfied with the current laws.

18. (D) Logic Reasoning (Parallel Reasoning)

Step 2: Identify the Question Type
The question asks for something in passage B that is "most analogous" to something mentioned in passage A, making this similar to a Parallel Reasoning question as often found in Logical Reasoning.

Step 3: Research the Relevant Text
The question refers to the relationship between comedians and copyright laws, which is described in the first paragraph. Copyright laws are said to be most relevant to the comedians' situation (lines 3–5), but the comedians don't use them (lines 5–8). Use this to find a logically similar argument made in passage B.

Step 4: Make a Prediction
Lines 44–46 present an exact parallel to the way comedians treat copyright laws. Like copyright laws in comedy, trade secrecy laws can be used by chefs. And like comedians, chefs opt not to use those laws. So, the relationship between comedians and copyright laws is parallel to that between chefs and trade secrecy laws.

Step 5: Evaluate the Answer Choices
(D) is correct.

(A) is a 180. Unlike how copyright laws do apply to jokes, passage B mentions how intellectual property laws do *not* typically apply to recipes (lines 40–43).

(B) is a 180. Unlike copyright laws, which do apply to jokes, patents generally do *not* apply to recipes (line 43).

(C) is a Distortion. This refers to the components of a recipe, which would be more comparable to the details of a joke, not the laws used to protect those jokes.

(E) is a 180. Copyright law is the legal system that comedians do *not* use. Social norms is the system that chefs *do* use.

19. (A) Inference

Step 2: Identify the Question Type
The question asks for something with which the author of passage A is "most likely to agree," making this an Inference question.

Step 3: Research the Relevant Text
The question does not refer to any specific idea, line, or paragraph, so the entire text of passage A is relevant.

Step 4: Make a Prediction
An exact prediction here is unlikely, if not impossible. Instead, go through the answers individually. Eliminate anything that is not consistent with the big picture, and use content clues in the choices to do any research, as necessary.

Step 5: Evaluate the Answer Choices
(A) is correct. The second paragraph suggests that, under conventional wisdom, one would expect the lack of legal recourse to deter creators because recouping costs is unlikely. However, the third paragraph is all about how social norms provide an effective alternative to legal recourse, helping comedians "maintain substantial incentives to invest in new material" (lines 37–38). This suggests that they can, indeed, recoup their costs using social norms.

(B) is a 180. Social norms are presented as an effective substitute, so there is no reason to expect the author to encourage using legal means more often.

(C) is Out of Scope and Extreme. Social norms may help reduce concerns about investing in new material, but that's not to say that comedians are completely unconcerned. Even if social norms do completely remove any concern for some comedians, there's no suggestion that this is true for *most* comedians.

(D) is Extreme. While social norms may be equally, if not more, effective for comedians, that doesn't mean this is true in general. Most other professions might be better served by law-based systems.

(E) is a Distortion. Although copyright laws don't seem to suit the needs of comedians, the author only addresses the use of social norms as an alternative. There is no indication that the author is interested in promoting legal reform.

20. (B) Logic Reasoning (Strengthen)

Step 2: Identify the Question Type
The question asks for something that would "support the argument" in passage B. That makes this a Strengthen question, like those in the Logical Reasoning section.

Step 3: Research the Relevant Text
For a Strengthen question, it helps to focus on the author's Main Idea, rather than spending time rereading the text.

Step 4: Make a Prediction

The author of passage B is arguing that social norms provide an effective means for chefs to protect their recipes. As evidence, the author merely describes the rules themselves. Unlike passage A, passage B never actually indicates any reason why chefs would follow those rules. If there were no consequences, the whole system would be meaningless. To strengthen this argument, the correct answer should provide an incentive to follow the rules, which would effectively support how this system could be considered effective.

Step 5: Evaluate the Answer Choices

(B) is correct. If violating the norms leads to one being denied information, that would provide a reason for chefs to follow the rules, making the system more likely to be effective.

(A) is irrelevant. The norms are meant to protect against chefs stealing recipes. It doesn't matter whether chefs can create similar recipes inspired by those recipes. At worst, this would weaken the argument because the lack of such a norm could actually encourage stealing recipes if chefs could just make one minor change and acceptably claim it to be "inspired" by the original.

(C) is a 180. If published recipes get legal protection, then there would likely be no need for the social norms system.

(D) is a 180. If the social norms system cannot be enforced, then there's no incentive to follow the rules, making the system utterly ineffective.

(E) is a 180. If it's impossible to make such a distinction, then it would be impossible to take action against a potential thief. The offending chef could just claim to have developed the recipe independently, and there would be no punishment. That would make the system ineffective.

Passage 4: Charlotte Perkins Gilman and Social Darwinism

Step 1: Read the Passage Strategically
Sample Roadmap

Line #	Keyword/phrase	¶ Margin notes
4	important	**Gilman & Social Darwinism**
7	but	
9	Some	
10	held	Side 1: Society is all biological evolution
11	strictly determined	
12	futile	Don't meddle
14	Another	
15	held; although	Side 2: Activist
18	need not	
19	but	Work together to change society
23	central thesis	Gilman agrees with side 2
24	although	We contribute to change society
31	not simply	
32	but was also	Ethical responsibility
33	argued	
35	primary	
39	not merely	Not just intellectual
41	vehemently	Gilman advicated change
42	especially	
43	In both	
44	urges	
46	central goal	
47	abandonment	Ex. urged women to fight gender roles
49	believed	
50	had been necessary	
53	believed	
53–54	now required	

Discussion

The very first sentence introduces Charlotte Perkins Gilman (**Topic**) and emphasizes the importance of her role in the debate about how Darwin's theories apply to society (**Scope**). The rest of the first paragraph outlines the two sides of the debate. Some Social Darwinists argue that society evolves strictly through biological evolution, and we shouldn't interfere with the competitive struggle for survival of the fittest. Others argue that biological evolution may play a partial role in changing society, but we help society evolve by actively working together rather than competing against one another.

In the second paragraph, the author mentions that Gilman sides with the second group, pushing the idea that humans can consciously contribute to the evolution of society. In fact, Gilman argues that it's an ethical responsibility, and people should use their personal skills to do work that's socially valuable.

In the third paragraph, the author claims that Gilman was not just making theoretical arguments. Instead, she actively encouraged people to change society. As an example, the author details Gilman's role in urging women to fight against traditional gender roles. They should abandon the outdated idea that certain jobs are gender-specific and work on restoring feminine qualities such as nurturing and cooperation to society.

The author does not take any sides, so the **Purpose** of the passage is to merely present information about Gilman. The **Main Idea** is that Gilman sided with those who felt Darwin's theories should encourage humans to actively help society evolve, as exemplified by her encouragement of women to fight against traditional gender roles.

21. (D) Global

Step 2: Identify the Question Type
The question asks for the "main point of the passage," making this a Global question.

Step 3: Research the Relevant Text
There's no need to go back into the text. Just consult the Main Idea as predicted while reading the passage strategically.

Step 4: Make a Prediction
The author's main point is that Gilman felt that humans should actively help society evolve, as evidenced by her encouraging women to fight against traditional gender roles.

Step 5: Evaluate the Answer Choices
(D) matches the author's main point.

(A) is a Distortion. Abolishing gender-specific work roles was just one facet of Gilman's activism, not the entire theory itself. Further, Social Darwinism served as a basis for her ideas, not the other way around, as this choice suggests.

(B) is Out of Scope. There is no indication that Gilman rejects any of the doctrines associated with the activist group of Social Darwinists.

(C) is Out of Scope and Extreme. The passage provides no evidence about how *most* Social Darwinists acted. And the passage is not about comparing Gilman's activities to that of other Social Darwinists.

(E) is Out of Scope. There is no suggestion that Gilman's writings on women's social issues were *not* widely recognized, and the author does not make it a point to recommend greater recognition.

22. (E) Inference

Step 2: Identify the Question Type
The question asks for something the passage "most strongly suggests," making this an Inference question.

Step 3: Research the Relevant Text
With no content clues or line references, the entire text is relevant.

Step 4: Make a Prediction
The correct answer could be based on any line or combination of details, so don't try to predict an exact response. Test the choices individually, using the big picture as a basis for comparison and using clues in the choices to do any necessary research.

Step 5: Evaluate the Answer Choices
(E) is correct. This is supported in lines 23–30, which suggest that there are Social Darwinists who, like Gilman, believe evolution has led us to a point where we can "contribute consciously" to our evolution and "mold our society in appropriate ways."

(A) is a 180. In line 21, the author directly states that Gilman's theories were allied with the activist group of Social Darwinists described in lines 14–20.

(B) is a 180. While there were some Social Darwinists who focused purely on biological issues (lines 9–14), there was already another group that focused on other issues (lines 14–20). Gilman aligned with those ideas; she didn't introduce them.

(C) is a Distortion. While Gilman is said to have identified with the other social activists, there's no indication that she collaborated with them directly.

(D) is Out of Scope. While the passage only mentions Gilman's connection to Social Darwinism, that doesn't mean they were the *only* influence on her work. It's very possible that she directly consulted Darwin's writings as well.

23. (A) Global

Step 2: Identify the Question Type

The question asks for the "organization of the passage" in its entirety, making this a Global question.

Step 3: Research the Relevant Text

Don't concentrate on the text of the passage. Instead, use the margin notes to get a sense of the purpose of each paragraph, from one stage of the passage to the next.

Step 4: Make a Prediction

The first paragraph describes the two sides of Social Darwinism. The author then discusses how Gilman aligns herself with one side of that debate (the activists). And the final paragraph shows how Gilman uses those beliefs to advocate for specific causes (e.g., fighting against gender roles). The correct answer will follow this structure, in general terms.

Step 5: Evaluate the Answer Choices

(A) is a match, with the identification of Gilman as a proponent of activist Social Darwinism, followed by a description of practical implications (Gilman's call for women to fight against gender roles).

(B) is Half-Right, Half-Wrong. It starts out fine, describing how Gilman's theories relate to the activist side of Social Darwinism. However, the author doesn't contrast Gilman's theories to other theories. And the author's tone is neutral in this passage. The author never rejects any theory.

(C) is Out of Scope. The author is neutral, merely describing Gilman's theories. The author never proposes an interpretation, nor does the author argue in favor of any interpretation.

(D) is a Distortion. The author does describe some reasoning by the activist Social Darwinists, but that's brought up as one side of a debate, which this choice omits. And the author never evaluates the reasoning. The author remains neutral throughout the passage.

(E) is Out of Scope, as the author provides no historical facts. Further, Gilman sided with activist Social Darwinism; she didn't formulate that theory herself. And the author never discusses critical response to her works.

24. (D) Detail

Step 2: Identify the Question Type

The question asks for something the passage *indicates*, making this a Detail question.

Step 3: Research the Relevant Text

The question asks for something mentioned as significant to the evolution of society. This matches the phrase "prime source of social evolution" in lines 33–34.

Step 4: Make a Prediction

Gilman argues that "human work, whether in crafts, trades, arts, or sciences" is important to social evolution.

Step 5: Evaluate the Answer Choices

(D) matches, as work in crafts, trades, etc., constitutes skilled occupations.

(A) is Out of Scope. There is no mention of "ancient social theories."

(B) is Out of Scope. The author never mentions communication among cultures.

(C) is Out of Scope. Literacy is never discussed in the passage.

(E) is Out of Scope. There is no mention of any methods used in social sciences, let alone dialectical ones.

25. (B) Detail

Step 2: Identify the Question Type

The question asks for something for which the "passage gives evidence." That means it will be directly stated, making this a Detail question.

Step 3: Research the Relevant Text

The question asks for something Gilman values as an "instrument of social progress," i.e., something used to promote social progress. The author describes her active promotion in the third paragraph.

Step 4: Make a Prediction

In lines 43–46, it's said that Gilman urged for social progress in "both her fiction and her social theory." So, she valued using fiction as an instrument, in addition to her theoretical arguments.

Step 5: Evaluate the Answer Choices

(B) is correct.

(A) is Out of Scope. There is no mention of industrialization, or any suggestion that it would be used to promote social progress.

(C) is Out of Scope. There is no mention of international travel.

(D) is Out of Scope. Religion plays no role in the passage or Gilman's theories as described.

(E) is a 180. Gilman sides with the activist group of Social Darwinists, who argue that society should *not* be competitive but should instead be collaborative (lines 18–20).

26. (B) Global

Step 2: Identify the Question Type

The question asks how the passage as a whole can "most accurately be described," making this a Global question.

Step 3: Research the Relevant Text

There's no need to go back into the text. Instead, consider the big picture and the Purpose of the passage.

Step 4: Make a Prediction

In this passage, the author is merely presenting the views of one theorist. The correct answer should stay this neutral without distorting any of the details.

Step 5: Evaluate the Answer Choices

(B) is correct. The passage merely describes Gilman's role and ideas as they relate to one side of the Social Darwinist debate.

(A) is Out of Scope. The author presents no opinion and thus never defends one side of a debate over another.

(C) is too narrow. The author does explain the basic points of both sides of Social Darwinism in the first paragraph, but this completely ignores the rest of the passage, which is focused primarily on Gilman and how her views fit within that debate.

(D) is Out of Scope. The author does not defend any point of view, nor is there any rejection of other interpretations.

(E) is a Distortion. The first paragraph does introduce Social Darwinism, but focuses on two views of that theory. And Gilman's views are not her own version of Social Darwinism. They are just aligned with an already established version that involves human activism.

27. (A) Inference

Step 2: Identify the Question Type

The question asks for something *implied* in the passage, making this an Inference question.

Step 3: Research the Relevant Text

Gilman's views are described throughout the second and third paragraph.

Step 4: Make a Prediction

There are a lot of views presented in the passage. Stick to the basic ideas (humans should be actively involved in helping society evolve; women should fight against established gender roles) to evaluate the choices, and use content clues to do any necessary research.

Step 5: Evaluate the Answer Choices

(A) is correct. It may have been difficult to find and/or predict, but it is supported by lines 46–56, which suggest that gender-specific roles were "at one time...necessary for evolution" (lines 49–50) but should now be abandoned to restore balance to society.

(B) is Extreme. While Gilman encourages collective action, there is no suggestion that this is the *only* way to bring about social evolution.

(C) is Out of Scope. There is no indication that Gilman finds the abandonment of gender-specific roles to be a difficult task.

(D) is a 180. Gilman directly states that the central thesis of Social Darwinism is "a source of ethical responsibility" (lines 32–33) and thus does have ethical implications.

(E) is Extreme. While Gilman encourages social evolution and believes that progress requires the inclusion of nurture and cooperation, there is no suggestion that this will *inevitably* occur.

Section III: Logical Reasoning

Q#	Question Type	Correct	Difficulty
1	Weaken	C	★
2	Flaw	E	★★
3	Assumption (Necessary)	C	★
4	Flaw	A	★
5	Strengthen	E	★
6	Role of a Statement	B	★
7	Point at Issue	A	★★
8	Strengthen	D	★
9	Assumption (Sufficient)	C	★
10	Inference	E	★★
11	Point at Issue	D	★
12	Inference	D	★★
13	Assumption (Sufficient)	E	★★
14	Inference	C	★★
15	Flaw	D	★★★★
16	Assumption (Necessary)	B	★★
17	Principle (Identify/Inference)	E	★
18	Assumption (Necessary)	A	★★
19	Principle (Identify/Strengthen)	D	★
20	Point at Issue	D	★
21	Inference	D	★★★★
22	Paradox (EXCEPT)	B	★★★
23	Parallel Reasoning	C	★★★
24	Strengthen	C	★★★
25	Assumption (Sufficient)	A	★★★
26	Parallel Flaw	D	★★★

1. (C) Weaken

Step 1: Identify the Question Type
The question directly asks for something that weakens the given argument.

Step 2: Untangle the Stimulus
The advertisement argues that tilapia is a perfect choice for people who want the health benefits of fish but don't like the taste of fish. The evidence is that tilapia doesn't taste fishy.

Step 3: Make a Prediction
The evidence definitely addresses the taste issue, but it never actually says that tilapia provides the desired health benefits. The advertisement assumes tilapia provides the same health benefits as other fish, and anything that suggests otherwise would weaken the advertisement's claim.

Step 4: Evaluate the Answer Choices
(C) is correct. If tilapia is an atypical fish that doesn't provide the touted health benefits, then it's not the "perfect choice" it's claimed to be.

(A) is Out of Scope. The advertisement is not trying to persuade people to eat more than is recommended, so such negative effects have no impact on the given claims.

(B) is also Out of Scope. The effect of tilapia on the environment has nothing to do with how it tastes or how eating it can be beneficial.

(D) is a 180, at worst. This just confirms that some people usually avoid eating fish because of the taste. If tilapia doesn't have the same fishy flavor, then it could indeed be perfect for such people.

(E) is irrelevant. Tilapia does not have the fishy flavor, so it doesn't matter how much people avoid foods that do have that flavor.

2. (E) Flaw

Step 1: Identify the Question Type
The question directly asks for a flaw in the given argument.

Step 2: Untangle the Stimulus
The author concludes (*therefore*) that the primary reason we developed language was to more easily domesticate animals. The evidence is that language provides the communication needed to domesticate animals.

Step 3: Make a Prediction
Just because language is used to domesticate animals doesn't mean that was the reason we developed language in the first place. That's like saying I could use a hammer to break open a walnut, so that must be why hammers were invented. The correct answer will describe this mistake of improperly treating one possible function of language as if that had to be the reason we developed language.

Step 4: Evaluate the Answer Choices
(E) is correct. Just because language serves a certain purpose (domesticating animals), it cannot be assumed that's why language developed in the first place.

(A) is a Distortion. The evidence does say that communication is necessary for domestication, but the author does not suggest or claim that communication guarantees domestication.

(B) is Out of Scope. The author does cite language as a means of bringing about domestication, but never suggests language is unique (i.e., the only thing that would have worked).

(C) is Out of Scope. There is no indication or suggestion that domestication and language developed around the same time.

(D) is not accurate. The conclusion and evidence are distinct. The conclusion is about the reason for language developing, while the evidence just describes a way language is used.

3. (C) Assumption (Necessary)

Step 1: Identify the Question Type
The question asks for an assumption that the "argument requires," making this a Necessary Assumption question.

Step 2: Untangle the Stimulus
The author concludes ([*t*]*hus*) that it's not always wrong or harmful to use others as a means to your own ends. The evidence is that many employers treat their employees fairly.

Step 3: Make a Prediction
There are a couple of Mismatched Concepts in this little argument. One of them is logical; if people are being treated *fairly* (as the employees are), then it's logical to suggest that they are not being treated in a morally reprehensible or harmful way. However, the conclusion is about people "using others as a means to one's own end." The evidence is only about what "[m]any employers" do, making no mention of them using their employees in such a manner. So, for this argument to work properly, the author must assume these mismatched concepts are connected, i.e., that there are employers who use others (their employees) as a means to their own ends.

Step 4: Evaluate the Answer Choices
(C) is correct. At least some employers must use their employees in such a manner. Using the Denial Test, if they didn't, then there would be absolutely no basis for the conclusion.

(A) is an Extreme Distortion. There is no suggestion about what constitutes "morally reprehensible" behavior, and it doesn't have to be *only* about harming others. If anything, the author argues that some employers don't act "morally reprehensibly *or* harmful," which suggests that morally reprehensible behavior probably *does* involve actions other than harm.

(B) is Extreme. The author only claims that *many* employers treat their employees fairly (and thus those employers act morally, despite treating their employees as a means to an end). That doesn't mean *no* companies who use employees as a means to an end act unfairly or in a reprehensible manner. There could be exceptions.

(D) is Extreme and Out of Scope. There's no indication that the employers in question are profiting. And even if they were, only *many* companies are said to be fair. There can still be some companies that are harming their employees.

(E) is an Extreme Distortion. The argument is not about what can cause harm, but whether there are actions that do *not* cause harm. Besides, there can be plenty of other ways to harm others that don't involve using them as a means to one's own end.

4. (A) Flaw

Step 1: Identify the Question Type
The correct answer is one that "describes a flaw" in the argument, making this a Flaw question.

Step 2: Untangle the Stimulus
The editorialist claims that we should not be alarmed by essays indicating the nation's decline. In other words, the nation is doing just fine. The evidence? The anxious tone of the essays is really just an indication of the writers' psychological state.

Step 3: Make a Prediction
The editorialist is blaming the writers for being anxious, but couldn't they be anxious because the nation is in decline? The editorial writer fails to consider this and tries to deflect attention away from the content of the essays by attacking the people who write the essays. This is a form of *ad hominem* attack, and the correct answer will describe the editorialist's attempt to ignore the actual content of the essays.

Step 4: Evaluate the Answer Choices
(A) is correct. The editorial writer dismisses the content of the essays based merely on those who wrote the essays, but offers no evidence that addresses the validity of the content.

(B) is a Distortion. There is only one situation presented: people writing essays saying the nation is in decline.

(C) is an Irrelevant Comparison. The editorialist just addresses the condition of the nation. There's no distinction between political or cultural issues.

(D) is Out of Scope. The editorialist doesn't say the nation is thriving. He just argues it's not in decline. He might very well accept that everything is just mediocre.

(E) is a 180. The editorial writer does dismiss the view that the nation is declining. However, he actually offers *no* evidence one way or the other. That's the problem. He merely attacks the people who wrote the essays.

5. (E) Strengthen

Step 1: Identify the Question Type
The question directly asks for something that strengthens the given argument.

Step 2: Untangle the Stimulus
The author argues that eating the spice turmeric can help prevent Alzheimer's disease. The evidence is that India has the highest rate of turmeric consumption and a relatively low rate of Alzheimer's. Also, turmeric contains curcumin, a compound that reduces the buildup of proteins associated with Alzheimer's.

Step 3: Make a Prediction
The author presents some great evidence, but the argument still rests on equating correlation with causation. The connection between turmeric consumption and low Alzheimer's rates in India is impressive but could still be coincidental. And the details about curcumin sound convincing, but turmeric could have other compounds that counteract the curcumin. In short, the author is assuming that turmeric does have a causal connection to Alzheimer's prevention, and the correct answer should provide yet another link that connects them.

Step 4: Evaluate the Answer Choices
(E) is correct. This bolsters the correlation in India, showing that Alzheimer's is lowest where curry consumption (and hence turmeric consumption) is highest.

(A) is a 180. This presents an overlooked possibility, suggesting that it could be rosemary or ginger, and not turmeric, that is responsible for the low rates of Alzheimer's in India.

(B) is a 180. This suggests that turmeric's ability to reduce the buildup of amyloid proteins won't help prevent Alzheimer's. If Alzheimer's is what causes the buildup, turmeric would only relieve the issue, not prevent it from occurring in the first place.

(C) is a 180. This suggests that the low levels of Alzheimer's in India might simply be because India has the lowest proportion of people old enough to be susceptible to the disease. So, the low rate of Alzheimer's is due to statistical probability, not consumption of turmeric.

(D) is irrelevant and, at worst, a 180. If other compounds in turmeric haven't been studied, then there's no additional evidence to connect turmeric to Alzheimer's prevention. Worse yet, if they were studied and found to *increase* amyloid production, that would work against the author's claims.

6. (B) Role of a Statement

Step 1: Identify the Question Type
The question provides a claim and asks for its "role in the...argument," making this a Role of a Statement question.

Step 2: Untangle the Stimulus
The official starts off by citing how people criticize the Forestry Department for taking too long to put out forest fires. *But*, the official refutes that by pointing out how small fires can actually be beneficial by clearing out potentially hazardous debris. *Therefore*, the official concludes it's actually good to let small fires burn.

Step 3: Make a Prediction
The question asks about the second sentence, in which the official mentions the benefit of how small fires can clear out unwanted trees and debris. The Keyword [b]ut indicates the official is using that claim to refute people's criticism against the Forestry Department. The claim is also used as evidence for the final conclusion about letting small fires burn. The correct answer will describe one or both of these purposes.

Step 4: Evaluate the Answer Choices
(B) is correct, as the second sentence is indeed used to counter the contention from the first sentence.

(A) is a 180. The Contrast Keyword [b]ut indicates the official is refuting the criticism against the Forestry Department, not supporting it.

(C) is a 180. If the critics had their way, the Forestry Department would put out fires more quickly. The claim in question shows why it's better to *not* put out fires immediately.

(D) is a Distortion and a 180. The claim in question is a general claim, not an example. Besides, it's used to counter what many people think, not illustrate or support it.

(E) is a Distortion. The Keyword [t]herefore indicates that the sentence about letting small fires burn is the conclusion. The claim in question is evidence to support that conclusion, not the other way around.

7. (A) Point at Issue

Step 1: Identify the Question Type
The question asks for something about which two speakers *disagree*, making this a Point at Issue question.

Step 2: Untangle the Stimulus
Gerald describes how anybody walking past another person's home can access the other person's Internet service, as long as it's not secured. Gerald argues this should not be illegal because it's similar to walking past someone listening to the radio and enjoying the music coming from that person's radio. Kendra counters by pointing out a problem with Gerald's analogy. In the radio situation, you're walking past someone and moving on. With the Internet, you'd have to stop moving and hang around for a while, which could constitute loitering or harassment.

Step 3: Make a Prediction
In short, Gerald finds accessing someone else's Internet service to be perfectly legitimate, while Kendra argues that there's a potential legal issue with it. The correct answer will address this question of legality.

Step 4: Evaluate the Answer Choices
(A) is correct. Gerald disagrees with this and suggests that accessing someone else's Internet service cannot be considered illegal, while Kendra says the opposite and argues it can be considered loitering or harassment, and thus illegal.

(B) is Out of Scope for Kendra. Kendra compares accessing someone else's Internet service to loitering and harassment, not trespassing. Kendra might very well agree with Gerald that it hardly constitutes trespassing.

(C) is a Distortion. Gerald and Kendra are arguing about whether accessing someone else's Internet service can be considered illegal, not whether it *should*.

(D) is Out of Scope for Gerald. Only Kendra mentions how accessing someone else's Internet service requires a lot of time. Gerald makes no mention of timing, and there's no indication he'd suggest otherwise.

(E) is Out of Scope. Neither Gerald nor Kendra talk about the possibility of unintentionally accessing someone else's Internet service.

8. (D) Strengthen

Step 1: Identify the Question Type
The question asks for something that "most strongly supports" the given argument, making this a Strengthen question.

Step 2: Untangle the Stimulus
The biologists are trying to explain why island plants are going extinct much more quickly than mainland plants. Their explanation is that, unlike mainland plants, island plants haven't developed defenses against large mammals eating them. The evidence is that islands are generally free of large mammals until humans move in.

Step 3: Make a Prediction
The biologist's explanation rests on assumed causality. The implication is that island plants are going extinct because they can't protect themselves against large, plant-eating mammals. However, there's no evidence that the extinction rate has any connection to the presence of large mammals. If island plants were rapidly going extinct *before* large mammals were around, then the biologists' explanation is illogical. To strengthen the argument, there needs to be some connection between the plant extinction rate and the appearance of land

mammals (which, by the evidence given, is connected to the appearance of humans—naturally).

Step 4: Evaluate the Answer Choices

(D) is correct. By the evidence given, large mammals are not present until humans arrive first. So, if the extinction rate rose dramatically after humans arrived, then the plants were surviving better before that happened, and hence before large mammals appeared. This doesn't prove that large mammals are responsible, but it definitely provides a more convincing connection.

(A) is an Irrelevant Comparison. It doesn't matter whether there are more surviving mainland plants or more surviving island plants. The argument is about *why* island plants are going extinct.

(B) is irrelevant. At best, this suggests that mainland plants are able to establish themselves on islands and survive, confirming that something is affecting island plants. However, it does not address the biologists' explanation and thus provides no additional support that the problem is due to a lack of defense against land mammals.

(C) is a 180. This offers an alternative explanation. If island plants are going extinct due to commercial development, then it may have nothing to do with a lack of defense against large mammals.

(E) is a potential 180. If large mammals prefer mainland plants, then they wouldn't eat as many island plants (provided mainland plants are available). In that case, the island plants don't have as much need for defense against large mammals, suggesting a different explanation for the high extinction rate.

9. (C) Assumption (Sufficient)

Step 1: Identify the Question Type

A fill-in-the-blank question is usually an Inference question. However, the blank in the stimulus here is preceded by the Keyword *since*, which indicates evidence. So, the blank is an unstated piece of evidence that would "most logically complete" the argument, making it a Sufficient Assumption question.

Step 2: Untangle the Stimulus

The conclusion being drawn at the end is that jokes are usually difficult to remember. The given evidence is that our brains respond best to patterns, as evidenced by how musical patterns can help us remember information that would otherwise be impossible to memorize.

Step 3: Make a Prediction

The only information given about jokes is that they elicit an emotional response, which is why they might *seem* easy to remember. But the author is arguing jokes are *not* easy to remember, so the emotional response is irrelevant. The only

relevant factor mentioned is patterns. If our brains respond best to patterns, then something without a pattern would be difficult to remember. So, to argue that jokes are difficult to remember, the author's argument is complete if she assumes that jokes don't have patterns.

Step 4: Evaluate the Answer Choices

(C) is correct. If jokes are designed to break patterns, then that goes against what's best for our brains. Thus, this provides the missing evidence for the author's claim that jokes are difficult to remember.

(A) is Out of Scope. There is no evidence that verbal or symbolic content is difficult to remember, so this offers no logical evidence for the conclusion.

(B) is a Distortion. Even if jokes vary in length, there could still be repeated patterns in how they are presented. Thus, there would still be no reason to suggest that they're difficult to remember.

(D) is a Faulty Use of Detail. This refers to the author's note that jokes elicit an emotional response. However, that was shown to be irrelevant, so this claim is equally irrelevant. Besides, it makes no mention of jokes and thus offers no reason to conclude that jokes are difficult to remember.

(E) is a Distortion. This confirms that patterns are better for the brain, but there's still no evidence that jokes lack patterns. Thus, this provides no evidence in support of the author's conclusion.

10. (E) Inference

Step 1: Identify the Question Type

The correct answer will be a claim that the given statements "most strongly support," making this an Inference question.

Step 2: Untangle the Stimulus

The author presents information about a prehistoric fish called Tiktaalik. This fish had fingers, which isn't as unusual as it may seem given how often prehistoric fish had variations. However, the fingers were important because the evolution of many animals with fingers can be traced back to Tiktaalik.

Step 3: Make a Prediction

There's not a lot of useful statements for making concrete deductions. The best that can be done is to summarize the basic idea and test the choices. In short, it's not unusual that Tiktaalik grew fingers, but that variation ultimately impacted evolution. The correct answer will stay consistent with this information without overstating any claims.

Step 4: Evaluate the Answer Choices

(E) is supported. Compared to other fish species of the time, the author claims that Tiktaalik would not have stood out as unusual. It's not until you compare it to modern land animals with fingers that the evolutionary impact is understood.

(A) is not supported. Tiktaalik is said to be an ancestor of animals that move on land, but there's no evidence that Tiktaalik itself ever got out of the water.

(B) is Extreme. The fingers are the only feature described in the stimulus, but there could be other features the author didn't mention.

(C) is Extreme. Even though Tiktaalik is an ancestor to many land animals, it could also be an ancestor to some fish, and there's no evidence otherwise.

(D) is Extreme. While fingers are presented as an evolutionary feature of many land animals, there can still be other ways fish can move on land that do not involve fingers.

11. (D) Point at Issue

Step 1: Identify the Question Type
The question asks for something about which two authors *disagree*, making this a Point at Issue question.

Step 2: Untangle the Stimulus
Gabriella argues that the government raising interest rates has slowed the country's economy by encouraging people to borrow less and thus spend less. Ivan disagrees (of course), claiming that the country's economy is merely mimicking the global economy, which itself has slowed down. *Therefore*, Ivan argues that the government is not responsible for the slowdown.

Step 3: Make a Prediction
Gabriella and Ivan agree that the country's economy has slowed down. The point at issue: Why? Gabriella blames the government for raising interest rates, while Ivan blames the global economy. The correct answer will address the debated cause of the slowdown.

Step 4: Evaluate the Answer Choices
(D) is correct. Gabriella would agree with this, saying that raising interest rates is the cause. Ivan directly says otherwise, that this is not the cause.

(A) is Out of Scope for Ivan. Gabriella states this, but Ivan does not address or contradict the claim that people are spending less.

(B) is Out of Scope for Gabriella and a Distortion for Ivan. Ivan claims that the country's economy is tied to the overall global economy, not to that of other countries in particular. Besides, Gabriella does not mention or suggest anything about how the country's economy relates to other economies.

(C) is Out of Scope for Ivan. He might agree with Gabriella that higher interest rates caused people to borrow less. However, his argument is solely about the end result: Did those higher rates cause an economic slowdown?

(E) is Out of Scope for Gabriella. Ivan mentions the global economy slowdown, but Gabriella has no stated or implied opinion about what's happening outside the country.

12. (D) Inference

Step 1: Identify the Question Type
The correct answer here will be chosen "on the basis of the statements" given, making this an Inference question. However, unlike most Inference questions, the correct answer here will be *rejected*, which means the statements will reveal it as false. That means the incorrect choices will be true or at least possible.

Step 2: Untangle the Stimulus
The author describes a scene in an ancient Greek play in which one character reads a prophecy written on a writing tablet. The character expresses amazement at what's written, but doesn't actually say what's written down until prompted by his companion.

Step 3: Make a Prediction
So, the character reads to himself, gasping in amazement until his companion says, "Hey, Demosthenes—care to share what's so mind-blowing?" (Roughly translated.) It's hard to predict exactly what this little scene will contradict, but look for an answer that is inconsistent with the actions that occur.

Step 4: Evaluate the Answer Choices
(D) is correct. Demosthenes does read to himself, rejecting the idea that people of that time did not do so.

(A) is Out of Scope. There's no indication of how a character would be identified as illiterate, so this could very well be true.

(B) is Out of Scope. There is no mention of the basis for the character of Demosthenes, so it's possible he's completely fictional.

(C) is a Distortion. While Demosthenes does start by reading the prophecy to himself, he eventually reads it aloud to the companion. Thus, there's no reason to reject the idea that such oral recitation is common.

(E) is a Distortion. While the prophecy was written down on a writing tablet in this case, there's no indication that this was a common occurrence. It still could have been a rare occurrence, and there's no logical reason to reject that idea.

13. (E) Assumption (Sufficient)

Step 1: Identify the Question Type
The question asks for something that "if...assumed," would logically complete the argument. That makes this a Sufficient Assumption question.

Step 2: Untangle the Stimulus
The author concludes in the final statement that human emotions are not physical phenomena. The evidence is that human emotions cannot be explained by science, particularly physics, chemistry, or neurophysiology.

Step 3: Make a Prediction

The author's argument is based on a Mismatched Concepts argument. The author uses evidence of scientific inadequacy to reach a conclusion that something is not physical.

Evidence:

| If | **human emotion** | → | **~ explained by science** |

Conclusion:

| If | **human emotion** | → | **~ physical phenomenon** |

The author assumes these concepts are connected:

| If | **~ explained by science** | → | **~ physical phenomenon** |

By contrapositive:

| If | **physical phenomenon** | → | **explained by science** |

Step 4: Evaluate the Answer Choices

(E) is correct, connecting the explanatory power of science to an item's physical nature.

(A) uses the right terms for the assumption, but gets the logic backward—using the conclusion to support the evidence. The author is not claiming that *all* nonphysical phenomena are unexplainable. The author is merely claiming that being unexplainable is the reason why one particular phenomenon (human emotion) is nonphysical. Science might be able to explain other nonphysical phenomena.

(B) is Out of Scope. Nothing is said to be felt by only one subject, and the argument doesn't claim emotions can't be studied. They just can't be explained.

(C) is an Irrelevant Comparison. The similarity of these three sciences has no bearing on whether human emotions are physical or not.

(D) is Extreme. This improperly suggests the author is assuming that everything is either physical or emotional. The author is merely suggesting that things can't be both physical and emotional, not that everything has to be one or the other. (Just like an animal cannot be both a cat and a dog, but not every animal has to be one or the other.)

14. (C) Inference

Step 1: Identify the Question Type

The correct answer will be something that the given information "most strongly supports," making this an Inference question.

Step 2: Untangle the Stimulus

The author provides a few observations based on some teeth marks found on *T. rex* skeletons: 1) The teeth marks could *only* be made by a large carnivore. 2) *T. rex* was the *only* large carnivore in its area. 3) The teeth marks indicate one of two things: combat or feeding. 4) Leaving teeth marks like that on a live animal would have been nearly impossible.

Step 3: Make a Prediction

Combining this information leads to an interesting implication. First off, if the teeth marks could only be made by a large carnivore, and *T. rex* was the only large carnivore in the area, that means the *T. rex* skeletons were bitten by another *T. rex*. These bites were caused by one of two actions: combat or feeding. But, it's nearly impossible to leave such a mark on a live animal, so the *T. rex* was likely dead when bitten, which means it wasn't in combat. That leaves option two: feeding. In other words, the dead *T. rex* was being eaten by another *T. rex*.

Step 4: Evaluate the Answer Choices

(C) is supported.

(A) is Out of Scope. The author only provides details about *T. rex* and the teeth marks found on *T. rex*. There's no indication how they interacted with other animals.

(B) is Out of Scope. While the evidence here suggests that one *T. rex* was eating another, that's not enough evidence to suggest this was common behavior for carnivores overall.

(D) is not supported. Although the teeth marks must have come from another *T. rex*, the marks being described were likely *not* made during combat. There may have been some *T. rex* versus *T. rex* combat (which didn't result in the teeth marks), but there's no support for that in the stimulus.

(E) is Out of Scope. The *T. rex* is said to be the only large carnivore in North America at the time. It's possible North America was the only location for large carnivores on Earth, and *T. rex* was the only one anywhere.

15. (D) Flaw

Step 1: Identify the Question Type

The question asks why the argument given is "vulnerable to criticism," which means there's a Flaw in the argument.

Step 2: Untangle the Stimulus

The author presents two views held by critics. First, they claim a poem is the only accurate expression of its own meaning, so poetry can never be accurately paraphrased. Second, the critics claim their own paraphrases are accurate. *Thus*, the author concludes that their first view (poetry cannot be accurately paraphrased) is false.

Step 3: Make a Prediction

Yes, the critics are contradicting themselves. They say a poem cannot be paraphrased accurately, but then they claim their own paraphrases are accurate. They can't have it both ways. The author recognizes that, but then arbitrarily decides that it's the *first* view that's wrong, i.e., poems *can* be paraphrased accurately. This overlooks the possibility that it's the *second* view that's wrong, i.e., the critics' paraphrases are just as inaccurate as anyone else's. The correct answer will describe this flaw of saying one view is false when it could be a second, equally problematic view that's false.

Step 4: Evaluate the Answer Choices

(D) is correct. The author denies the critics' first view (poems cannot be accurately paraphrased) without any explanation why that view is any less acceptable than the other view (the critics' paraphrases are accurate).

(A) describes Circular Reasoning, which is not being used here. The author refutes a view by assuming the truth of a different view, not just assuming the original view was always wrong.

(B) is an Irrelevant Comparison. The author does not differentiate between information and feelings, so there's no reason to assume that conveying information is more important than conveying feelings, or vice versa.

(C) is Out of Scope. The author is not questioning how useful a paraphrase is, just whether the paraphrase can be accurate or not.

(E) is not a flaw. There's no reason for the word *paraphrase* to have multiple meanings in this argument, so there's nothing wrong with assuming one consistent definition.

16. (B) Assumption (Necessary)

Step 1: Identify the Question Type

The question asks for an assumption on which the argument *depends*, making this a Necessary Assumption question.

Step 2: Untangle the Stimulus

Critics complain that a tax bill providing incentives for large companies is reducing tax revenues. *Yet*, the author counters them by arguing that the tax bill has created a lot of jobs. The author's evidence is that a company, Plastonica, opened a factory in the area that qualified for the tax bill incentives and led to 75 employees being hired.

Step 3: Make a Prediction

The author is confusing correlation with causation. The Plastonica factory happened to open and employ new people after the tax bill had passed, but was the tax bill really responsible for that? The author overlooks the possibility that Plastonica may have been planning to open that factory all

along, and the tax bill was a nonissue. The author must assume that the tax bill played some causal role in the factory's opening.

Step 4: Evaluate the Answer Choices

(B) is correct, suggesting the tax bill incentives were the reason for Plastonica opening its factory. By the Denial Test, if Plastonica would have opened the factory without the incentives, then the tax bill would be irrelevant, contrary to the author's claim. The author must assume otherwise: that Plastonica would *not* have opened the factory.

(A) is not necessary. This suggests that Plastonica specifically wanted to open in the author's area and nowhere else. In that case, perhaps the author has a point and the tax bill was influential. However, this does not have to be true. Even if Plastonica would have opened a factory elsewhere, it still could have been swayed by the tax bill. The potential of opening elsewhere has no bearing on the author's argument.

(C) is Out of Scope. The argument is not about whether the bill will create more jobs in the future or how many people believe that. The author's argument is that the bill has already created jobs, and this has no bearing on that.

(D) is irrelevant. This just suggests that Plastonica was determined to open a factory and just happened to choose the author's area. That doesn't mean the tax bill had anything to do with the decision.

(E) is irrelevant. It doesn't matter what the critics believe. The author has statistical evidence of jobs being created, so the author's argument is not affected by whatever critics believe.

17. (E) Principle (Identify/Inference)

Step 1: Identify the Question Type

The question asks for a *generalization* illustrated by the specific situation described, making this an Inference-based Identify the Principle question.

Step 2: Untangle the Stimulus

In the situation described, customers complained when a gas station started charging 25 cents extra to customers who paid by credit card. In response, the gas station raised the price of gas and instead gave a 25-cent discount to customers who paid by cash. And people were happy with this.

Step 3: Make a Prediction

This situation is all about psychological manipulation. In either case, people who pay by credit card are paying 25 cents more than people who pay by cash. It's just that people complain when the price difference is described as one group paying extra, but they're perfectly content when it's described as one group getting a discount. It's all about how the message is communicated. The correct answer will conform to this idea that people's perception of a situation can change by merely presenting it in a different way.

Step 4: Evaluate the Answer Choices

(E) is correct. In this case, people were not evaluating the situation itself because the situation doesn't actually change—there's still a 25-cent price difference. Instead, they were evaluating the situation based on the presentation: Saying one group has to pay extra is bad, but saying one group gets a discount is okay.

(A) is Out of Scope and Extreme. There is no evidence that people are acting without careful assessment of the evidence. Perhaps they do, logically, realize that the price difference hasn't changed. However, they still could bristle at how it's presented. Furthermore, there's no indication this is how people *usually* behave.

(B) is a 180, at worst. The people who pay by credit card are apparently happy when the price difference is presented as a discount for people paying cash. However, there's still no benefit to using a credit card, so those customers are not basing their judgment on personal benefit.

(C) is a Distortion and Extreme. The situation is meant to show what can cause people's emotions to switch, not whether financial situations *usually* make people emotional.

(D) is Out of Scope and Extreme. There's no indication whether or not this issue is significant in people's lives. Additionally, it's just one instance, so it would be improper to say people *often* change their minds about such issues.

18. (A) Assumption (Necessary)

Step 1: Identify the Question Type

The question asks for "an assumption required" by the argument, making this a Necessary Assumption question.

Step 2: Untangle the Stimulus

The herbalist notes that it can take several months for herbal medicines to work optimally. However, daily doses of such medicines for too long can be toxic. *Therefore*, the herbalist concludes that some people taking daily doses should skip occasional doses to avoid toxicity.

Step 3: Make a Prediction

The herbalist has a valid concern. However, the toxicity is said to occur after a long period of time. Even though it takes a long time for herbal medicines to work best, there's no evidence that people actually use such medicine for that long. The recommendation to skip doses would be necessary only if the herbalist assumes people are taking the medicine long enough to be toxic.

Step 4: Evaluate the Answer Choices

(A) must be assumed. If nobody uses herbal medicines long enough to experience side effects, then there's no reason to skip doses. The herbalist must assume such long-term usage.

(B) is irrelevant. The herbalist's argument is about avoiding negative side effects. It doesn't matter if skipping doses makes the medicine more or less effective. As long as people aren't poisoned, the herbalist's argument stands.

(C) is Out of Scope. The existence of medicines that could be toxic even when skipping daily doses is not required for the herbalist's recommendation to be valid. Some people could still benefit from skipping doses on medicines that are *not* toxic if doses are skipped.

(D) is Extreme. The herbalist is not advocating that *anyone* who uses herbal medicines should use them for months. The herbalist is just urging caution for *some* people who may.

(E) is Extreme. While the herbalist's argument is based on potential toxicity, that's not to say this is the *only* reason why people might want to skip the occasional dose. The herbalist might have other reasons for skipping that are not presented here.

19. (D) Principle (Identify/Strengthen)

Step 1: Identify the Question Type

The correct answer will be a principle, making this an Identify the Principle question. Moreover, the principle "most helps to justify" the given argument, making this work similar to a Strengthen question.

Step 2: Untangle the Stimulus

According to the business owner, there is one section of the city in which food trucks are taking up metered parking spaces, making traffic worse. In reaction, the city council is looking to ban food trucks from using metered parking spaces in *any* commercial area of the city. The business owner argues the bill should be rejected because most areas of the city don't have the same problem.

Step 3: Make a Prediction

The business owner is unhappy with the city council's overly broad solution. The food truck problem is only in one area, while most areas are unaffected. The business owner is acting on the principle that problems in one area need not be solved by restricting *all* areas, especially if most areas are not affected by that problem.

Step 4: Evaluate the Answer Choices

(D) is correct. This applies exactly to the council's bill, which would disadvantage food trucks throughout the city even though the problem they cause in one area has no effect in most other areas.

(A) is Out of Scope. There's no evidence that the food trucks are not valued by consumers.

(B) is a 180. The city council is trying to address the problem, but the business owner is rejecting its solution.

(C) is Out of Scope. There is no indication whether the current problem has been thoroughly studied or not.

(E) is Out of Scope. The business owner is not rejecting the policy because it will aggravate the problem. It would probably solve the problem, but just put too much restriction elsewhere.

20. (D) Point at Issue

Step 1: Identify the Question Type
The question asks for a point about which two speakers *disagree*, making this a Point at Issue question.

Step 2: Untangle the Stimulus
Michele is against companies overhauling their databases because it's usually more trouble than it's worth. Alvaro, on the other hand, suggests that overhauling a database is fine as long as it's done right.

Step 3: Make a Prediction
The point at issue is whether or not overhauling a database is a good idea. Michele says no, while Alvaro says yes, as long as it's done right.

Step 4: Evaluate the Answer Choices
(D) is correct. Michele says not to overhaul, as the problems aren't worth it. Alvaro says otherwise. The best advice is to overhaul, but be sure to do it right.

(A) is Out of Scope. Neither speaker address *why* companies would want to overhaul a database.

(B) is Extreme. Alvaro is not saying that problems *never* outweigh the rewards. Alvaro would likely agree with Michele that problems *could* outweigh the rewards, if the process is done improperly.

(C) is Out of Scope. Neither Michele nor Alvaro distinguish between different types of overhauls.

(E) is Out of Scope. Michele does not address recoding a database, and Alvaro never suggests that professional experience is necessary. It just requires doing the job right, experience or no experience.

21. (D) Inference

Step 1: Identify the Question Type
The question asks for something that "must...be true" based on the given information, making this an Inference question.

Step 2: Untangle the Stimulus
The author describes an experiment in which people were shown a series of images on a computer screen, some at the top of the screen and some at the bottom. When asked to guess where the next image would be, they all claimed to see some kind of pattern, but they guessed incorrectly more often than correctly. Meanwhile, they would have been correct more often than not if they just said "top" every time.

Step 3: Make a Prediction
The author claims that the images *usually* appeared at the top and, if they had guessed "top" every time, subjects would have been correct most of the time. So, most of the images

(i.e., more than half) appeared at the top. Similarly, less than half the people's guesses were correct, so most of the images were guessed incorrectly. If most images were on top, and most were guessed wrong, then it logically follows that some were both; i.e., some were on top when people guessed wrong. You can use some numbers to verify this. Say there were 10 images. If most were on top, that's at least 6. And if people guessed right less than half the time, the best they did was 4 right and 6 wrong. Of the 4 they got right, that couldn't possibly include all 6 images that appeared on top. So, some of the images on top had to be ones people guessed wrong (i.e., they guessed it was going to be on the bottom).

Step 4: Evaluate the Answer Choices
(D) must be true.

(A) is potentially a 180. If they always guessed "top," they may have based that decision on a perceived pattern in which images appear at the top far more often than on the bottom.

(B) is a Distortion. First, the question asks for something that *must* be true. What happened in this experiment is not necessarily applicable to decision-making in general, so this cannot be said to be absolutely true. Besides, the more successful method described is always guessing the same result, not always guessing based on what just happened.

(C) is Extreme. The subjects all claimed to see a pattern that ultimately did not exist, but that doesn't mean there was *no* predictable pattern.

(E) is Extreme. While always guessing "top" would have been a better strategy than the one subjects used, it's not necessarily the *most* rational strategy. There may have been a pattern that subjects did not perceive that would have produced even better results.

22. (B) Paradox (EXCEPT)

Step 1: Identify the Question Type
The question asks for something that "helps to resolve the apparent paradox," making this a Paradox question. The EXCEPT indicates that four choices will resolve the paradox. The correct answer will not. It will either deepen the mystery or have no effect on it whatsoever.

Step 2: Untangle the Stimulus
It's always 10 degrees colder in Taychester than in Charlesville, but the average person in Charlesville spends more on heating during the winter.

Step 3: Make a Prediction
Take a moment to paraphrase the mystery: If it's always 10 degrees warmer in Charlesville, why are people there spending more on heating? There could be countless reasons: Heating is just more expensive there, people are more sensitive to cold weather there, etc. Don't bother predicting

every possible explanation. Four choices will provide a distinction about Charlesville that would affect people's heating expenditures. The correct answer will not describe a difference or will describe one that's irrelevant to heating.

Step 4: Evaluate the Answer Choices
(B) is correct. Even if Charlesville had wild temperature swings, it is always 10 degrees warmer than Taychester. Taychester would thus experience the same temperature swings, which means there's still no resolution to why Charlesville spends more on heat than Taychester.

(A) would resolve the issue. Heat loss due to wind is greater in Charlesville, so they would need to use more heat to compensate.

(C) would resolve the issue. Heating is just more expensive in Charlesville, so residents could wind up paying more even if they use less heat.

(D) would resolve the issue. People in Charlesville have warmer weather while people in Taychester have colder weather. If people with warmer weather tend to keep their houses warmer in the winter, that could explain why Charlesville residents are spending more.

(E) would resolve the issue. Charlesville residents would have to use more heat because their homes are not as well insulated.

23. (C) Parallel Reasoning
Step 1: Identify the Question Type
The question asks for an argument with reasoning "most similar to that" in the given argument. That makes this a Parallel Reasoning question.

Step 2: Untangle the Stimulus
The argument presents two pieces of data about cars at Rollway Motors. All new cars cost more than $18,000, and all cars at least 10 years old cost less than $5,000. Thus, the author concludes that any car that costs between $5,000 and $18,000 is used and less than 10 years old.

Step 3: Make a Prediction
The logic here is solid. Consider the Formal Logic of the first two statements. First, all new cars cost more than $18,000. So, if it's new, it costs more than $18,000.

If	**new**	→	**> $18,000**

Next, all cars at least 10 years old cost less than $5,000. So, if it's at least 10 years old, it costs less than $5,000.

If	**10+ years old**	→	**< $5,000**

So, what if a car costs something in the middle? Consider the contrapositives. If it's not more than $18,000, it cannot be

new. And if it's not less than $5,000, it cannot be at least 10 years old.

If	**~ > $18,000**	→	**~ new**
If	**~ < $5,000**	→	**~ 10+ years old**

So, any car in the middle price range must not be in either group: It's not new, and it's not at least 10 years old. The correct answer will follow similar logic. Provide a high range for one group of items, a low range for another group of items, and suggest that anything in the middle range is not part of either group.

Step 4: Evaluate the Answer Choices
(C) is a match. It provides a high range for one group of items (every apartment above the fourth floor must have three or more bedrooms) and a low range for another group (every apartment below the fourth floor must have less than two bedrooms). The author then concludes that any item in the middle range (two bedrooms—no more, no less) cannot be part of either original group (not above the fourth floor, and not below—it must be *on* the fourth floor).

If	**5th floor and up**	→	**3+ bedrooms**
If	**3rd floor and down**	→	**< 2 bedrooms**

Conclusion:

If	**~ 3+ AND ~ < 2 (exactly 2)**	→	**~ 5th floor and up AND ~ 3rd floor and down (just the 4th floor)**

(A) does not match. This does separate two sets of apartments: Those above the fourth floor all have more than two bedrooms, and those below the fourth floor all have less than two bedrooms. However, this doesn't use the contrapositive as the original argument did. Instead, this just negates the logic without reversing it. The original argument did not say that all used cars under 10 years old were in the mid-price range, so it's not parallel for this argument to say *all* fourth floor apartments have exactly two bedrooms.

(B) is logical, but does not match the original. The original argument presented two groups in a high and low range (above $18,000 and below $5,000) and made a conclusion about the middle ground (between $5,000 and $18,000). This argument has two ranges (two to three bedrooms and two or fewer bedrooms), but no middle ground because there's overlap between the two ranges.

(D) does not match. It doesn't provide two ranges to draw a conclusion about items in the middle ground. Instead, this adds an additional factor of balconies that is not parallel to anything in the original.

(E) is logical, but doesn't match because it does not provide two ranges to draw a conclusion about items in the middle ground. Instead, it brings up vacant apartments, which are not parallel to anything in the original.

24. (C) Strengthen

Step 1: Identify the Question Type
The question asks for something that "provides the most support" for the given argument, making this a Strengthen question.

Step 2: Untangle the Stimulus
Despite the greater number of tornadoes reported since the 1950s, the meteorologist argues that the actual number of tornadoes has *not* increased. The evidence is that we're just better at finding them now.

Step 3: Make a Prediction
The meteorologist is essentially making a causal argument: More reports are caused by an increased ability to *find* tornadoes, not an actual increase in tornadoes. To strengthen that argument, the correct answer should provide additional evidence that numbers have remained constant while finding ability has improved.

Step 4: Evaluate the Answer Choices
(C) is correct. If large and medium tornadoes have stayed constant, then the increase in reports is exclusively from small tornadoes, which are likely to be harder to find than bigger ones. This suggests that we are getting better at finding tornadoes and that rates for tornadoes of certain sizes are constant, as the meteorologist assumes.

(A) is Out of Scope. The argument is about the number of reports and the number of tornadoes, not the amount of damage inflicted.

(B) is a 180, at worst. Perhaps there are just more major population centers or an improbable increase in tornadoes only near population centers. However, it's also possible that it suggests there *are* more tornadoes overall. So, this does not support the meteorologist.

(D) is Out of Scope or a potential 180. If the death rate is rising, then it could very well be that there are more

tornadoes, contrary to the meteorologist's claim. At best though, the discussion of tornado deaths is immaterial to arguing about the number of tornadoes.

(E) is irrelevant. It doesn't matter where the tornadoes strike. Even if the geographic range hasn't changed, there could still be more tornadoes in that range, contrary to the meteorologist's assertion.

25. (A) Assumption (Sufficient)

Step 1: Identify the Question Type
The question asks for something that, "if...assumed," would complete the argument. That makes this a Sufficient Assumption question.

Step 2: Untangle the Stimulus
The salesperson argues that handheld vacuums are likely to be good enough for people with small uncarpeted areas. The evidence is that such vacuums are easy to use and work just fine on wood and tile floors.

Step 3: Make a Prediction
Great! Handheld vacuums work well on wood and tile. However, the conclusion is about uncarpeted areas, not specifically wood and tile. What if most people have other uncarpeted areas: concrete, glass, marble, etc.? The salesperson overlooks those possibilities and assumes that uncarpeted floors are pretty much limited to wood and tile.

Step 4: Evaluate the Answer Choices
(A) is correct. If most consumers use only carpet, wood, and tile, then uncarpeted areas will be mostly wood and tile, matching the salesperson's assumption.

(B) is irrelevant. The salesperson never says handheld vacuums are *not* good on carpeting. And besides, even if they are, that doesn't confirm that they're good enough for uncarpeted floors.

(C) is a Distortion. Good handheld vacuums don't *all* have to be inexpensive. And even if they were, that doesn't mean that most such vacuums are good enough for wood and tile, as the salesperson suggests.

(D) is Out of Scope. The salesperson is not claiming that everyone with uncarpeted areas has vacuuming needs. The argument is based solely on people who do have vacuuming needs.

(E) is Out of Scope. The argument is about whether inexpensive handheld vacuums are good enough for certain jobs. The salesperson is not concerned with how much other, more versatile vacuums might cost.

26. (D) Parallel Flaw

Step 1: Identify the Question Type
The question asks for an argument that "most closely parallels that" in the given argument. Furthermore, that

reasoning is said to be flawed, making this a Parallel Flaw question.

Step 2: Untangle the Stimulus

The author presents two pieces of logic: 1) If global warming is to be halted, we need to decrease reliance on fossil fuels, and 2) if there were incentives to use alternative energy, reliance on fossil fuels would decrease. *So*, the author concludes that halting global warming requires those incentives.

Step 3: Make a Prediction

The author commits the flaw of confusing necessity and sufficiency. Look at the Formal Logic: 1) If global warming is halted, reliance on fossil fuels must decrease.

If	halt global warming	→	decrease reliance on fossil fuels

2) If incentives are in place, reliance decreases.

If	incentives	→	decrease reliance on fossil fuels

However, while decreasing our reliance on fossil fuels is necessary to halt global warming, incentives are not required to decrease that reliance. The incentives are merely sufficient, not necessary. Algebraically, the author argues this: If X → Y; if Z → Y; thus, if X → Z. The correct answer must commit the same exact flaw: present one requirement (decrease reliance on fossil fuels), suggest a sufficient condition to bring about that requirement (incentives), and improperly conclude that the sufficient condition is required.

Step 4: Evaluate the Answer Choices

(D) is a match. The author presents a requirement (we need to keep good teachers) and suggests a sufficient condition to bring about that requirement (improve salaries). The author then improperly concludes that improving salaries (a sufficient condition) is necessary.

(A) is not flawed. This presents two pieces of logic and strings them together properly. Ending unemployment leads to ending poverty, which in turn ends hunger. Perhaps this view is a little simplistic, but it does not have the same logical flaw as the original.

(B) does not match. This does commit the flaw of confusing necessity with sufficiency. However, unlike the original argument, the two pieces of logic here can be connected:

If	exercise	→	good health	→	happy life

Here, the author's argument is If X → Y; if Y → Z; thus, if Y → X. The conclusion totally omits the concept of "happy life," and it just reverses (without negating) the first piece of evidence. So, like the original, this argument does misinterpret Formal Logic, but it does not do so in a similar or parallel way.

(C) does not match because it is not flawed. The two pieces of logic can be connected:

If	pro job	→	college	→	high school

Then, the conclusion properly identifies high school as necessary for getting a professional job. No flaw.

(E) does not match. Unlike the original argument, the two pieces of evidence can be connected:

If	prevent abuse	→	expand educ. efforts	→	increased cooperation

Then, the author takes a necessary condition (increased cooperation) and treats it as a sufficient condition to make a prediction. Essentially, the author's argument is If X → Y; if Y → Z; thus, if Z → X. That requires improperly reversing both pieces of Formal Logic, not just one as the original argument did.

Section IV: Logic Games

Game 1: Travel Agent Tour of Asian Cities

Q#	Question Type	Correct	Difficulty
1	Acceptability	D	★
2	"If" / Must Be True	C	★
3	Could Be True EXCEPT	B	★★
4	"If" / Must Be True	B	★
5	"If" / How Many	C	★★

Game 2: Student Concert Performance

Q#	Question Type	Correct	Difficulty
6	"If" / Could Be True	D	★
7	Could Be True	B	★
8	Must Be False (CANNOT Be True)	E	★★★
9	Must Be False (CANNOT Be True)	A	★★★
10	"If" / Must Be True	E	★★
11	"If" / Must Be True	B	★

Game 3: Railway System Closures

Q#	Question Type	Correct	Difficulty
12	Acceptability	D	★
13	"If" / Must Be True	E	★
14	Could Be True	D	★★
15	"If" / Could Be True EXCEPT	B	★
16	"If" / Must Be True	D	★★★
17	Rule Substitution	A	★★★★

Game 4: Office Tower Air Quality Examinations

Q#	Question Type	Correct	Difficulty
18	Partial Acceptability	E	★★★
19	Could Be True	A	★★★
20	Could Be True EXCEPT	C	★★
21	Completely Determine	E	★★★★
22	"If" / Must Be True	D	★★★
23	Rule Substitution	A	★★★★

Game 1: Travel Agent Tour of Asian Cities

Step 1: Overview
Situation: A travel agent arranging a tour

Entities: Six cities (Hanoi, Jakarta, Manila, Osaka, Shanghai, Taipei)

Action: Selection/Sequencing Hybrid. Determine which cities will be included in the tour (Selection) and the order in which the selected cities will be visited (Sequencing).

Limitations: Exactly four cities will be included, and each city will be visited exactly once.

Step 2: Sketch
List the entities by initial and set up an In/Out sketch. Draw four numbered slots in the In column and two unnumbered slots in the Out column.

$$H \; J \; M \; O \; S \; T$$

$$\underline{\quad} \; \underline{\quad} \; \underline{\quad} \; \underline{\quad} \; \Big| \; \underline{\quad} \; \underline{\quad}$$
$$1 \quad 2 \quad 3 \quad 4 \qquad out$$

Step 3: Rules
Rule 1 establishes Hanoi and Taipei as included. It also sets a restriction that they cannot be visited consecutively. To notate their selection, circle H and T in the entity list and/or list them underneath the In column. Then, to the side, make a note that they cannot be consecutive, in either order.

$$\boxed{\cancel{HT}} \quad \boxed{\cancel{TH}}$$

Rule 2 presents some Formal Logic. If Osaka is included, then Shanghai is not. By the contrapositive, if Shanghai is included, then Osaka is not.

$$O \rightarrow \sim S$$
$$S \rightarrow \sim O$$

In short, if one of those cities is selected, the other cannot be selected. In other words, the tour cannot include both. So, at least one of them (if not both) will be left off the itinerary. Add O/S to one of the Out slots, keeping in mind that it's possible for both cities to be left out.

Rule 3 sets a restriction on Jakarta. If it's included, it must be visited third.

That doesn't mean it will be visited. It could still be left out. However, it does mean Jakarta cannot be visited first, second, or fourth. It also means that if any other city is visited third, Jakarta will not be on the tour.

$$J \rightarrow \frac{J}{3}$$
$$\frac{\text{other city}}{3} \rightarrow \sim J$$

Rule 4 is more Formal Logic. If Jakarta and Manila are both included, they will be consecutive.

$$J \; \& \; M \rightarrow \boxed{JM} \text{ or } \boxed{MJ}$$

The contrapositive of such a rule is rather convoluted and not very helpful: If they're not consecutive, then they're not both included. This is a rare case in which drawing out the contrapositive is not necessary.

Step 4: Deductions
With three of the rules based on Formal Logic, most deductions cannot be made until certain conditions are met. In addition, there are only five questions, three of which are If questions. These factors suggest that there will be few, if any, valuable deductions to be found.

If anything, the Duplication of Jakarta in the last two rules serves as a source of Limited Options. In one option, Jakarta would be included, and hence be third (Rule 3). In the second option, Jakarta would be left out.

In the first option, Jakarta would be third. By Rule 1, Hanoi and Taipei are also included, but cannot be consecutive, i.e., they cannot be first and second here. So, one of them will be fourth. That affects the last rule. If Manila is also included, it could only be second (to be consecutive with Jakarta). But there's no guarantee Manila is included, so that's all this option provides.

$$\textcircled{H} \; \textcircled{J} M \; O \; S \textcircled{T}$$

$$\underline{\quad} \; \underline{\quad} \; \underset{3}{\overset{J}{\underline{\quad}}} \; \underset{4}{\overset{H/T}{\underline{\quad}}} \; \Big| \; \underset{out}{\overset{O/S}{\underline{\quad}}} \; \underline{\quad}$$
$$\underset{1}{} \quad \underset{2}{}$$
$$\underset{T/H}{\searrow \; \swarrow}$$

In the second option, Jakarta is left out, along with either Osaka or Shanghai (Rule 2). That means everything else is included: Hanoi, Manila, Taipei, and either Osaka or Shanghai (whichever one is not out). At that point, Hanoi and Taipei need to be separated, but they could be first and third, first and fourth, or second and fourth, in any of those orders. None of the remaining cities is restricted, so the order is wide open.

$$\begin{array}{c} \text{(H)} \cancel{J} \text{(M)} \ O \ S \text{(T)} \\ \underline{} \ \underline{} \ \underline{} \ \underline{} \ \Big| \ \begin{array}{cc} O/S & J \\ \end{array} \\ 1 \quad 2 \quad 3 \quad 4 \quad \quad out \\ \text{H, T, M, O/S} \end{array}$$

Step 5: Questions

1. (D) Acceptability

As with any Acceptability question, go through the rules individually and eliminate choices as they violate the rules.

(E) violates Rule 1 by omitting Hanoi from the tour. **(C)** violates Rule 2 by including Osaka but also including Shanghai. **(A)** violates Rule 3 by having Jakarta visited first. **(B)** violates Rule 4 by including Jakarta and Manila, but not having them consecutive. That leaves **(D)** as the correct answer.

2. (C) "If" / Must Be True

For this question, Shanghai is included and is visited fourth. Hanoi and Taipei are also included and cannot be consecutive (Rule 1), so they must be visited first and third, in either order. That leaves the second slot on the tour. By the contrapositive of Rule 2, including Shanghai on the tour means Osaka is left out. And Jakarta cannot be visited second (Rule 3). That leaves Manila as the only city that could be visited second.

$$\begin{array}{c} \underline{H/T} \ \underline{M} \ \underline{T/H} \ \underline{S} \ \Big| \ \begin{array}{cc} O & J \\ \end{array} \\ 1 \quad 2 \quad 3 \quad 4 \quad \quad out \end{array}$$

That makes **(C)** the correct answer.

3. (B) Could Be True EXCEPT

Four of the choices here could be true. The correct answer will be the exception, the one that cannot be true (i.e., must be false).

If Jakarta is included, it must be third. In that case, it's certainly possible for Hanoi to be second, with Taipei fourth and either Osaka or Shanghai first. This could be true, eliminating **(A)**.

If Jakarta is included, it must be third. If Manila is also included, it cannot be fourth. Otherwise, that would leave Hanoi and Taipei to be first and second, violating Rule 1. So, Manila would have to be second, before Jakarta, not after. That means **(B)** is impossible, making it the correct answer.

$$\begin{array}{c} \underline{H/T} \ \underline{T/H} \ \underline{J} \ \underline{M} \ \Big| \ \begin{array}{cc} \cancel{O} & S \\ \end{array} \\ 1 \quad 2 \quad 3 \quad 4 \quad \quad out \end{array}$$

For the record, the remaining answers are all seen as possible in sketches for other questions. Osaka is included but not visited third in the fifth question, eliminating **(C)**. Manila is

immediately between Hanoi and Taipei in both the correct answer to the Acceptability question as well as the sketch for the second question, eliminating **(D)**. And one of the sketches for the fifth question has two cities between Hanoi and Taipei, eliminating **(E)**. Even **(A)** could be quickly confirmed as possible in the sketch for the fourth question.

4. (B) "If" / Must Be True

For this question, Manila is not included in the tour. By Rule 2, either Osaka or Shanghai must also be left out. That means the tour must include the remaining cities: Hanoi, Jakarta, Taipei, and either Osaka or Shanghai (whichever one is not left out). Jakarta would have to be third (Rule 3). Hanoi and Taipei cannot be consecutive (Rule 1), so they cannot be first and second. One of them will be fourth. The other will be first or second, with Osaka or Shanghai taking up the remaining spot.

$$\begin{array}{c} \underline{} \ \underline{} \ \underline{J} \ \underline{H/T} \ \Big| \ \begin{array}{cc} O/S & M \\ \end{array} \\ 1 \quad 2 \quad 3 \quad 4 \quad \quad out \end{array}$$

The only definite is that Jakarta is third, making **(B)** correct. **(D)** is impossible, and the remaining answers are all possible but need not be true.

5. (C) "If" / How Many

For this question, Osaka is included and is second. By Rule 2, that means Shanghai is out. Hanoi and Taipei are included, but cannot be consecutive, which means they cannot be third and fourth here. So, one of them is first. The other is third or fourth. Because the question asks for the total number of possible outcomes for the fourth city, draw two sketches to be thorough.

In the first, Hanoi and Taipei are visited first and third, in either order. That leaves Jakarta or Manila for the fourth city. However, Jakarta cannot be fourth (Rule 3), so it must be Manila.

$$\begin{array}{c} \underline{H/T} \ \underline{O} \ \underline{T/H} \ \underline{M} \ \Big| \ \begin{array}{cc} S & J \\ \end{array} \\ 1 \quad 2 \quad 3 \quad 4 \quad \quad out \end{array}$$

In the second sketch, Hanoi and Taipei are visited first and fourth, in either order. That leaves Jakarta or Manila for the third city.

$$\begin{array}{c} \underline{H/T} \ \underline{O} \ \underline{J/M} \ \underline{T/H} \ \Big| \ \begin{array}{cc} S & M/J \\ \end{array} \\ 1 \quad 2 \quad 3 \quad 4 \quad \quad out \end{array}$$

With that, the fourth city could be Manila (in the first sketch), or either Hanoi or Taipei (in the second sketch). That's three possible cities, making **(C)** correct.

Game 2: Student Concert Performance

Step 1: Overview

Situation: A music professor planning a concert

Entities: Five students (Gloria, Hazel, Roberto, Sonja, Toshiro)

Action: Loose Sequencing. Determine the order in which the students perform. The designation of this game as "loose" can only be determined by looking ahead to the rules. The rules only define relative ordering, with no mention of specific positions or spacing between entities.

Limitations: Each student performs once, and one at a time, so the sequencing is standard one-to-one.

Step 2: Sketch

List the entities by initial. The sketch for a Loose Sequencing game involves a tree diagram that shows the connections between entities, so there's no need to draw a series of slots.

G H R S T

Step 3: Rules

Rule 1 establishes Hazel at some point earlier than Roberto.

H—R

Rule 2 presents some Formal Logic. If Gloria performs earlier than Toshiro, then Roberto and Sonja also perform earlier than Toshiro. By contrapositive, if either Roberto or Sonja does not perform earlier than Toshiro (i.e., if one of them performs later than Toshiro), then Gloria performs later than Toshiro.

$$G-T \longrightarrow \begin{array}{c} R \\ S \end{array} \!\!> T$$

$$T-R/S \longrightarrow T-G$$

Rule 3 sets up two options: Either Hazel performs earlier than both Sonja and Toshiro or Hazel performs later than both Sonja and Toshiro.

$$H <^{S}_{T} \text{ or } S >^{H}_{T}$$

Step 4: Deductions

The last rule provides two outcomes for three of the five students, making it the perfect basis for Limited Options. In the first option, Hazel performs earlier than both Sonja and Toshiro (who could perform in either order).

In the second option, Hazel performs later than Sonja and Toshiro (again, in either order). With the Duplication of Hazel in Rule 1, add Roberto after Hazel in both options.

That leaves Rule 2. In the first option, Gloria could still perform earlier or later than Toshiro, so Gloria cannot be added. Instead, keep the Formal Logic handy to apply it when necessary.

$$\text{I)} \quad H \begin{array}{c} \nearrow R \\ - S \\ \searrow T \end{array} \quad G?$$

In the second option, Toshiro performs earlier than Hazel, and thus earlier than Roberto. Because Roberto does not perform earlier than Toshiro, Gloria cannot perform earlier than Toshiro. So, Gloria must perform later than Toshiro, with no connection to anyone else.

$$\text{II)} \quad \begin{array}{c} S \\ \searrow \\ T \end{array} \!\! H - R \\ \searrow G$$

Step 5: Questions

6. (D) "If" / Could Be True

For this question, Gloria performs first. Because it establishes a position, draw a series of slots and add G to the first position. With G in the first position, that means Gloria performs earlier than Toshiro, so Roberto and Sonja must also perform earlier than Toshiro (Rule 2). Hazel must perform earlier than Roberto (Rule 1), which is earlier than Toshiro performs. So, Hazel will also perform earlier than Sonja (Rule 3). Because Hazel performs earlier than everyone else who's left, Hazel will perform second. With Roberto and Sonja both performing earlier than Toshiro (Rule 2), Toshiro must perform fifth. Robert and Sonja will perform third and fourth, in either order.

G	H	R/S	S/R	T
1	2	3	4	5

With that, only **(D)** is possible and thus the correct answer.

If you had used the Limited Options, placing Gloria first is only possible in Option I. Then, from the Option I sketch, it is clear that Hazel must be second. However, be careful not to forget about applying Rule 2, which is what forces Toshiro into the fifth spot.

7. (B) Could Be True

The correct answer to this question will be a pair of students that could perform first and second, in that order. The incorrect choices will list students that cannot be first and second, respectively.

By Rule 2, if Gloria performs first and thus earlier than Toshiro, then Roberto and Sonja must also perform earlier than Toshiro. It would be impossible for Toshiro to be second in that case, eliminating **(A)**. (This is confirmed in the first question, which places Gloria first, resulting in Toshiro performing fifth.)

If Hazel and Gloria were first and second, respectively, then Gloria would perform earlier than Toshiro. That means Roberto and Sonja would also perform earlier than Toshiro, making Toshiro perform last. Robert and Sonja would be third and fourth, in either order.

$$\frac{H}{1} \quad \frac{G}{2} \quad \frac{R/S}{3} \quad \frac{S/R}{4} \quad \frac{T}{5}$$

This is possible, making **(B)** correct. For the record:

Hazel must perform earlier than Roberto, which means Roberto cannot be first, eliminating **(C)**. And if Roberto were second, Hazel, not Sonja, would have to be first, eliminating **(D)**. Finally, if Toshiro were first and Hazel second, Hazel would perform earlier than Sonja. That means Hazel would perform later than Toshiro but earlier than Sonja, violating Rule 3. That eliminates **(E)**.

8. (E) Must Be False (CANNOT Be True)

The correct answer here will be two students who cannot be fourth and fifth, in that order (i.e., that cannot be, in the order provided, the last two performers). The remaining choices will all list possible pairs of students for the last two performances, in order.

Instead of testing each choice individually, look for ways to test multiple choices simultaneously. Two choices list Toshiro as fifth and two list Roberto as fifth. Start by testing those conditions.

If Toshiro is fifth, then Hazel performs earlier than Toshiro, so Hazel will also perform earlier than Sonja (Rule 3) and Roberto (Rule 1). Gloria can perform anywhere without affecting the rules, as Roberto and Sonja are already performing earlier than Toshiro.

$$\frac{}{1} \quad \frac{}{2} \quad \frac{}{3} \quad \frac{}{4} \quad \frac{T}{5}$$

$$H \begin{cases} R \\ S \end{cases} G?$$

In that case, the fourth performer could be any of Gloria, Roberto, or Sonja. **(A)** and **(C)** are thus possible and can be eliminated.

If Roberto performs fifth, then Roberto cannot perform earlier than Toshiro. By Rule 2, Gloria cannot perform earlier than Toshiro, so Gloria must perform later than Toshiro.

$$\frac{}{1} \quad \frac{}{2} \quad \frac{}{3} \quad \frac{}{4} \quad \frac{R}{5}$$
$$\qquad\qquad\qquad \underset{\sim T}{}$$
$$T-G$$

In that case, it's impossible for Toshiro to be fourth, making **(E)** correct. For the record:

When Roberto is fifth, Hazel could perform at any time earlier than that. And if Hazel performs later than Sonja and Toshiro, Hazel could perform fourth, eliminating **(B)**. And Sonja and Gloria could perform fourth and fifth. In that case, Gloria would perform later than Toshiro, making Rule 2 irrelevant. Hazel could then perform first, earlier than everyone else. That's acceptable, eliminating **(D)**.

$$\frac{H}{1} \quad \frac{R/T}{2} \quad \frac{T/R}{3} \quad \frac{S}{4} \quad \frac{G}{5}$$

9. (A) Must Be False (CANNOT Be True)

The correct answer here will be two students who cannot be second and third, in that order. The remaining choices will all list students that could be second and third, respectively.

Here, each choice lists a different student in each position. There's no way of testing multiple answers simultaneously. This is worth skipping temporarily in favor of drawing sketches for the subsequent New-"If" questions. Doing so can help eliminate choices, reducing the amount of time needed to work on this question. As it turns out, the sketch for the first question of the game indicates that Hazel and Roberto could be second and third, respectively. That eliminates **(B)**. And in the sketch for the last question of the game, Roberto could be second with Toshiro third. That eliminates **(C)**. While that still leaves three choices to test, that will take less time than testing all five.

Thankfully, the first choice leads to an immediate problem. If Gloria and Hazel performed second and third, then Roberto would perform later (Rule 1), either fourth or fifth. The first performance would be Sonja or Toshiro. However, that would mean Hazel performs later than just one of them. The other would perform later, forcing Hazel to perform later than one but earlier than the other.

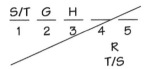

This violates Rule 3, making **(A)** correct. (This can also be seen using the Limited Options. Hazel could only be third in the second option, but that would require Sonja and Toshiro to be first and second, with no room for Gloria second.) For the record:

Sonja and Gloria could perform second and third. In that case, Hazel could perform first, earlier than Roberto, Sonja, and Toshiro. And with Gloria performing earlier than Toshiro, Toshiro could perform last so that Roberto and Sonja also perform earlier than Toshiro.

$$\frac{H}{1} \quad \frac{S}{2} \quad \frac{G}{3} \quad \frac{R}{4} \quad \frac{T}{5}$$

That's possible, eliminating **(D)**. And Toshiro and Sonja could perform second and third. In that case, Sonja performs later than Toshiro, so Gloria must, too (Rule 2). Gloria would thus be fourth or fifth. That leaves Hazel and Roberto. Hazel would perform first, with Roberto in fourth or fifth.

$$\frac{H}{1} \quad \frac{T}{2} \quad \frac{S}{3} \quad \frac{G/R}{4} \quad \frac{R/G}{5}$$

This is acceptable, eliminating **(E)**.

10. (E) "If" / Must Be True
For this question, Sonja performs first. Hazel will have to perform later than Sonja, so Hazel will also have to perform later than Toshiro (Rule 3), but earlier than Roberto (Rule 1), creating the string T...H...R.

$$\frac{S}{1} \quad \frac{}{2} \quad \frac{}{3} \quad \frac{}{4} \quad \frac{}{5}$$
$$T-H-R$$

With Roberto performing later than Toshiro, Gloria cannot perform earlier than Toshiro (Rule 2), so she will perform later than Toshiro, too. With all remaining students performing later than Toshiro, Toshiro must perform second.

$$\frac{S}{1} \quad \frac{T}{2} \quad \frac{}{3} \quad \frac{}{4} \quad \frac{}{5}$$
$$H-R; G$$

That makes **(E)** correct. The remaining choices are all possible but need not be true.

11. (B) "If" / Must Be True
For this question, Sonja performs fifth. That means Hazel must perform earlier than Sonja, so Hazel must also perform earlier than Toshiro (Rule 3). Sonja will also perform later than Toshiro, so Gloria cannot perform earlier than Toshiro (Rule 2) and hence must perform later than Toshiro. That means, in order, Hazel will perform earlier than Toshiro, who will perform earlier than Gloria. Hazel must also perform earlier than Roberto (Rule 1).

$$\frac{H}{1} \quad \frac{}{2} \quad \frac{}{3} \quad \frac{}{4} \quad \frac{S}{5}$$
$$H-T-G$$
$$\searrow R$$

So, Hazel performs earlier than everyone and thus performs first.

That makes **(B)** correct. **(C)** is impossible, and the remaining choices are all possible but need not be true.

Game 3: Railway System Closures

Step 1: Overview

Situation: A railway system operator closing some stations

Entities: Six stations (L, M, N, P, Q, R)

Action: Selection. Determine which stations the operator chooses to close.

Limitations: At least one station will be closed. There's no maximum, so it's possible that all six stations could be closed.

Step 2: Sketch

For most Selection games in which the numbers are not set, it's suggested to merely list a roster of the entities. Then, if an entity is selected, circle it. If it's not selected, cross it out. However, for this game, the "selected" entities will be "closed," which means the unselected entities will be "open." It might be confusing to circle the closed stations and cross out the open ones. So, it might be clearer to set up an In/Out sketch with the columns labeled "closed" and "open." At least one station will be closed, so start with one slot in the "closed" column and that's all.

$$\text{closed} \mid \text{open}$$
$$\overline{\quad\quad}$$

Step 3: Rules

Rule 1 prevents N and R from both being closed. In other words, at least one of them will remain open. Perhaps both remain open, but that's not certain. For now, add N/R to the "open" column.

Rules 2 and 3 provide Formal Logic. If N stays open, so does L, and if R stays open, so does M. Be sure to form the contrapositive of both. If L does not stay open (i.e., if L is closed), then N does not stay open (i.e., N is closed). And similarly, if M is closed, then so is R.

Rule 4 prevents L and R from both staying open. In other words, at least one of them will be closed. Perhaps both are

closed, but that's not certain. For now, add L/R to the "closed" column.

Step 4: Deductions

The Duplication of R in three of the rules indicates that R will be the most significant entity of the game. Whether R is open or closed makes a big difference, so it's best to set up Limited Options.

In the first option, R will stay open. By Rule 3, that means M will also stay open. Also, with R open, L cannot also stay open (Rule 4), so L will be closed. By Rule 2, that means N must also be closed. That leaves stations P and Q, neither of which is mentioned in any of the rules. They are Floaters. And, because the minimum requirement of one closed station has already been met, P and Q can stay open or be closed without affecting any other station.

$$
\begin{array}{c|c}
\text{I)} & \text{closed} \mid \text{open} \\
& \dfrac{L}{N} \quad \dfrac{R}{M} \\
& \uparrow \qquad \uparrow \\
& \quad P, Q
\end{array}
$$

In the second option, R will be closed. By Rule 1, N cannot also be closed, so N will stay open. By Rule 2, that means L will also stay open. With L open, Rule 4 prevents R from staying open, but that's already given. That leaves Rule 3, which only applies if R stays open. With R closed, the sufficient condition is not met, so there's no deduction to be made about M. It could be closed or open. Finally, as in Option I, stations P and Q are Floaters.

$$
\begin{array}{c|c}
\text{II)} & \text{closed} \mid \text{open} \\
& \dfrac{R}{} \quad \dfrac{N}{L} \\
& \uparrow \qquad \uparrow \\
& M, P, Q
\end{array}
$$

Step 5: Questions

12. (D) Acceptability

As with any Acceptability question, go through the rules one at a time and eliminate choices that violate the rules. Just keep in mind that the choices list stations that remain open, not ones that close.

(A) violates Rule 1 because, if L and M are the only stations open, then N and R would both be closed. **(C)** violates Rule 2 by having N open but not L. **(B)** violates Rule 3 by having R open but not M. **(E)** violates Rule 4 by having L and R both open. That leaves **(D)** as the correct answer.

13. (E) "If" / Must Be True

For this question, exactly five of the six stations stay open. That means only one is closed. Looking at the Limited Options, that can only happen if R is closed. If R is open, then L is closed (Rule 4), which means N is also closed (Rule 2). That would be two stations closed. So, if only one station is closed, it must be R, making **(E)** correct.

14. (D) Could Be True

The correct answer will list two stations that could both be closed. The remaining choices will list pairs of stations that cannot both be closed.

Note that three choices list R and three choices list M. That means it's possible to test three answers simultaneously rather than testing each answer individually. And with Limited Options based on R, it makes sense to test what happens if R is closed.

Per Option II, if R is closed, then N cannot be closed and thus must be open (Rule 1). With N open, L will also be open (Rule 2). So, L and N cannot be closed when R is closed, eliminating **(B)** and **(E)**. However, when R is closed, there's no restriction on M. So, M could also be closed, making **(D)** possible and thus the correct answer. In fact, this is consistent with the contrapositive of Rule 3: If M is closed, then R would also be closed. And if M is closed and thus R is closed, L and N would both be open (as described for Option II—the only option when M can be closed). So, L and N couldn't be closed when M is closed, either. That confirms that **(A)** and **(C)** can be eliminated.

15. (B) "If" / Could Be True EXCEPT

For this question, L will be open. By Rule 4, R cannot also stay open and thus must be closed. That means, by Rule 1, N cannot also be closed, so N must stay open. This is the result seen in Option II, with R closed. In that case, M could be open or closed and there's no way to know about P or Q for certain.

closed	open
R	L
	N

However, N is open and cannot be closed, making **(B)** correct.

16. (D) "If" / Must Be True

For this question, exactly two stations will stay open, which means exactly four will be closed. This could happen in either option (with R open or closed), so test them both.

If R is open, then so is M (Rule 3). That would mean everything else (L, N, P, and Q) would be closed. This does not violate any rules.

I) closed	open
L	R
N	M
P	
Q	

If R is closed, then N cannot be closed (Rule 1), so N would be open. That means L would also be open (Rule 2). That's two stations open, so everything else (M, P, Q, and R) would be closed.

II) closed	open
R	N
M	L
P	
Q	

In both options, Q is among the closed stations, so Q must be closed, making **(D)** correct. The remaining choices list stations that could be open in one of the two options.

This question can also be answered quickly with the Limited Options. Because Option I and Option II each already have two closed stations, everything else would be closed in either option. That means for both options, the Floaters—P and Q—would have to be among the stations that must be closed.

17. (A) Rule Substitution

The correct answer to this question will be a rule that, if substituted for Rule 3, will have the exact same effect on the game. In other words, it will provide the exact same restriction without adding any new restrictions.

The rule being replaced requires M to be open when R is open. The correct answer should be another condition that requires M to be open, and only **(A)** does that. Start by testing that to confirm it works. When R is open, by Rule 4, L cannot also be open, so L would be closed. So, if the rule "If L closes, then M must stay open" is added, keeping R open would close L and thus lead to M staying open. That would create the exact same effect that the original rule provided, confirming **(A)** as the correct answer. For the record:

(B) and **(C)** are consistent with the original rules. If L closes, then N must close (Rule 2), which means R cannot also be closed (Rule 1), so R must stay open. And if R closes, then N cannot be closed (Rule 1), so N must be open, which means L must be open. However, neither of these conditions would restore the rule about M staying open.

And **(D)** and **(E)** add new restrictions that are not warranted. By the original rules, if L is open then R must be closed (Rule 4), which then means N cannot be closed (Rule 1). However, M could have been open or closed in that case, so there's no reason to force it to be closed. And if M was open, the original rules provided no restrictions. So, a rule requiring N to be closed in that case would be unnecessarily restrictive.

Game 4: Office Tower Air Quality Examinations

Step 1: Overview

Situation: An environmental consultant scheduling examinations of the air quality in an office tower

Entities: Eight floors, from the first floor to the eighth

Action: Strict Sequencing. Determine the order, from Wednesday to Saturday, in which the floors will be examined. It may have been tempting to call this a Distribution game (assign the floors to the days of examination), but it's crucial to see the days as sequential, given how most of the rules indicate which floors are examined "earlier" than others. And why not call it a Distribution/Sequencing Hybrid? In short, the label "Hybrid" suggests multiple actions. Distribution/Sequencing would involve first distributing the entities into subgroups, then creating individual sequences for each group. In this game, there is only one action: assign the floors to days, which happen to be sequential. In the end, it doesn't matter what you call it. The sketch would likely be the same no matter what: a column for each day, with spaces to assign the floors. And that's going to be more important than placing an exact label on the game.

Limitations: Each floor is examined on just one day, and exactly two floors are examined each day.

Step 2: Sketch

List the floors by number (1–8), and set up four columns for the four days (W, T, F, S). Place two slots under each day.

```
    W   T   F   S
    __  __  __  __

    __  __  __  __
```

Step 3: Rules

Rule 1 puts a restriction on each day. The two floors on any given day must be separated by at least one other floor. In other words, there cannot be consecutively numbered floors on any given day. (For example, floors 2 and 3 cannot be examined on the same day.) Make a note of this to the side.

No consecutive floors
on same day
e.g. 1̸
      2̸

Rules 2, 3, and 4 set up loose orderings for three sets of floors: The second floor is examined on an earlier day than the eighth floor, the third floor is examined on an earlier day than the seventh floor, and the seventh floor is examined on an earlier day than the fifth floor. Rules 3 and 4 can immediately be combined.

2...8
3...7...5

Rule 5 limits the fourth floor to either Thursday or Friday. Draw a 4 below the sketch with arrows pointing to Thursday and Friday.

Step 4: Deductions

From the rules, a lot of floors are restricted. From Rule 2, the second floor cannot be examined on Saturday (as it must be examined before the eighth floor). Similarly, the eighth floor cannot be examined on Wednesday.

From Rules 3 and 4, the third floor has to be examined earlier than the seventh floor, which has to be examined earlier than the fifth floor. So, the third floor cannot be examined on Friday or Saturday. The seventh floor cannot be examined on Wednesday or Saturday. And the fifth floor cannot be examined on Wednesday or Thursday.

These restrictions, along with Rule 5, limit four of the floors to just two possible options. The third floor can only be on Wednesday or Thursday. The fourth floor can only be on Thursday or Friday. The fifth floor can only be on Friday or Saturday. And the seventh floor can only be on Thursday or Friday. Any one of these situations can potentially be used to set up Limited Options. With the third floor as a basis, one option is very fruitful, and that option is tested directly on the second question. Similarly, using the fifth floor as a basis provides one great sketch, which is directly tested on the fifth question. Basing options on the fourth floor yields a couple of worthy deductions, while basing options on the seventh floor yields the least amount of info. None of these Limited Options is necessary to manage the game effectively, but they are worth considering if they make it easier to understand the implications of the rules.

It is worth noting that the first and sixth floors are Floaters. They are not mentioned in any of the rules, and are thus among the least restricted entities.

Step 5: Questions

18. (E) Partial Acceptability

For a Partial Acceptability question, start by testing the rules individually as if it were a standard Acceptability question. Eliminate any choices that directly violate the rules. If there are any remaining choices, consider the entities and positions that are not listed, and test that information against the rules.

(B) violates Rule 1 by having the second and third floors examined on the same day. **(C)** violates Rule 5 by having the fourth floor examined on Wednesday.

For the remaining answers, consider what's missing. Each answer lists only Wednesday and Thursday, so any remaining floors will have to be assigned to Friday and Saturday. **(A)** lists the first, third, sixth, and eighth floors. That means the second, fourth, fifth, and seventh floors would be examined on Friday and Saturday. However, that violates Rule 2 because the second floor would be examined later than the eighth (which is tested on Thursday). That eliminates **(A)**.

(D) lists the second, fourth, sixth, and eighth floors. That means the first, third, fifth, and seventh floors must be examined on Friday and Saturday. However, that violates the combination of Rules 3 and 4. By Rule 3, the third floor must be examined earlier than the seventh floor, so the third floor would be examined on Friday and the seventh floor on Saturday. That would then leave no room for the fifth floor to be examined later than the seventh floor. That eliminates **(D)**, leaving **(E)** as the correct answer. For the record, **(E)** lists the second, third, sixth, and seventh floors. That means the first, fourth, fifth, and eighth floors would be examined on Friday and Saturday. The fourth floor would have to be examined on Friday (Rule 5), forcing the fifth floor to be examined on Saturday (Rule 1). The first and eighth floors could then be assigned to either day without violating any rules.

19. (A) Could Be True

For this question, the third floor will be examined on Thursday. The seventh floor has to be examined later in the week (Rule 3), but still has to be examined earlier in the week than the fifth floor (Rule 4). So, the seventh floor has to be examined on Friday, and the fifth floor has to be examined on Saturday.

The fourth floor has to be examined on Thursday or Friday, but cannot be examined on Thursday with the third floor (Rule 1), so it must be examined on Friday. Friday is fully scheduled.

W	T	F	S
	3	7	5
		4	

The second floor has to be examined earlier than the eighth floor, so it cannot be examined on Saturday. Friday is filled, and it cannot be examined on Thursday with the third floor (Rule 1), so it must be examined on Wednesday. That leaves the first, sixth, and eighth floors. The first floor cannot be examined on Wednesday with the second floor (Rule 1), nor can the eighth floor (Rule 2). Thus, the only remaining option for Wednesday is the sixth floor. The first and eighth floors will be examined on Thursday and Saturday, in either order.

W	T	F	S
2	3	7	5
6	1/8	4	8/1

With that, only **(A)** is possible and is thus the correct answer.

20. (C) Could Be True EXCEPT

The four incorrect choices all could be true. The correct answer will be the exception, the one that cannot be true (i.e., must be false).

None of the rules restrict the first or sixth floors—the Floaters—so it certainly seems possible for the first to be examined on Friday or the sixth to be examined on Saturday. In fact, the first floor could be examined on Friday in the correct answer to the first question, and in the sketch for the fifth question, it's possible to have the sixth floor examined on Saturday. That eliminates **(A)** and **(D)**.

The question stem for the second question of the game establishes the third floor on Thursday, so that surely could be true, eliminating **(B)**.

The fifth floor has to be examined later than the seventh floor (Rule 4), which in turn has to be examined later than the third floor (Rule 3). Thus, the fifth floor cannot be examined until Friday, at the earliest. It cannot be examined on Thursday, making **(C)** correct. For the record:

The eighth floor could be examined on Friday in the correct answer to the first question. That eliminates **(E)**. This illustrates how challenging non-"If" questions can often be handled deftly after sketches have been drawn for other questions. Feel free to skip these early on and come back to them later. That said, in some situations like this one, the correct answer is merely a quick deduction that comes from making the negative deductions about the placement of the 3...7...5 chain. So, if the question is answered quickly, proceed with it, but if you get stuck on it, wait until you have previous work to help you eliminate answers.

21. (E) Completely Determine

The correct answer will provide a piece of information that leads to a single possible outcome for all eight floors. The remaining answers will allow for at least two possible outcomes.

Using sketches from other questions can be very useful here. For the second question of the game, the sketch has the third floor on Thursday. However, it cannot be determined whether the first floor is examined on Thursday and the eighth floor on Saturday, or vice versa. With two possible outcomes, this eliminates **(B)**.

For the fifth question, the sketch has the second floor and the fifth floor on Friday. However, the first and sixth floors can be examined on Wednesday and Saturday in either order. Again, with two possible outcomes, this eliminates **(A)** and **(C)**.

That leaves two choices to test. The sixth floor is a Floater, so placing it in the sketch is not going to directly impact any other floors. That makes **(D)** unlikely, so it's better to start with **(E)**. If the eighth floor is examined on Thursday, the second floor would have to be examined on Wednesday (Rule 2). The third floor has to be examined earlier than the seventh floor (Rule 3), which in turn has to be examined earlier than the fifth floor (Rule 4). So, the third floor has to be examined on Wednesday or Thursday, but cannot be on Wednesday with the second floor (Rule 1). So, the third floor is examined on Thursday, with the seventh floor examined on Friday and the fifth floor examined on Saturday. With Thursday filled, the fourth floor must be examined on Friday (Rule 5). That leaves the first floor and the sixth floor. The first floor cannot be examined on Wednesday with the second floor (Rule 1), nor can the sixth floor be examined on Saturday with the fifth floor (Rule 1). So, the first floor and the sixth floor must be on Saturday and Wednesday, respectively.

W	T	F	S
2	8	7	5
6	3	4	1

The sketch is completely determined, making **(E)** the correct answer. For the record:

If the sixth floor is examined on Thursday, it's possible to deduce that the seventh floor is examined on Friday and the fifth floor is examined on Saturday. However, the first, second, third, fourth, and eighth floors could all be assigned on different days. There are too many outcomes, thus eliminating **(D)**.

22. (D) "If" / Must Be True

For this question, the fifth floor is examined on Friday. By Rules 3 and 4, the seventh floor must be examined on an earlier day, and the third floor must be examined earlier than that. So, the third floor must be examined on Wednesday and the seventh floor on Thursday. The fourth floor couldn't be examined on Friday with the fifth floor (Rule 1), so it must be examined on Thursday (Rule 5). Thursday is now filled up. The second floor has to be examined earlier than the eighth floor (Rule 2), so it cannot be examined on Saturday. It also cannot be examined on Wednesday with the third floor (Rule 1), so it must be examined on Friday. That means the eighth floor must be examined on Saturday. That leaves the first floor and the sixth floor, neither of which is impacted directly by the rules. They will be examined on Wednesday and Saturday, in either order.

W	T	F	S
3	7	5	8
1/6	4	2	6/1

With that, the second floor must be on Friday, making **(D)** the correct answer.

23. (A) Rule Substitution

The correct answer to this question will be a rule that perfectly replaces Rule 5 (the fourth floor is examined on Thursday or Friday). That means it must reestablish the original condition without adding any new restrictions. The incorrect answers will either fail to establish the fourth floor on Thursday or Friday or they will add restrictions that weren't originally presented.

(A) tries to limit the fourth floor by placing it on the same day as or immediately before or after the seventh floor. The seventh floor must be examined later than the third floor (Rule 3) and earlier than the fifth floor (Rule 4), which means it can only be examined on Thursday or Friday. This might seem to allow the fourth floor to be examined on Wednesday or Saturday, but it actually doesn't. If the seventh floor is examined on Thursday, then the third floor would be examined on Wednesday, preventing the fourth floor from being examined that day (Rule 1). So, the fourth floor would have to be examined on Thursday (the same day as the seventh floor) or Friday (the next day). Similarly, if the seventh floor is examined on Friday, the fifth floor would be examined on Saturday, preventing the fourth floor from being examined that day (Rule 1). So, the fourth floor would have to be examined on Thursday (the day before the seventh floor is examined) or Friday (the next day). Either way, the original rule is restored: The fourth floor is limited to Thursday or Friday, with no further restrictions. That makes **(A)** the correct answer. For the record:

If the fourth floor cannot be examined earlier than the second floor, then it could be examined on a later day...or on the very same day. So, this rule would allow the fourth floor to be examined on Wednesday with the second floor, which was not originally allowed. That eliminates **(B)**.

If the fourth floor has to be examined before the fifth floor, it couldn't be evaluated on Saturday, but it could still be examined on Wednesday. That was not originally allowed, so eliminate **(C)**.

(D) sets up a conditional statement based on the fourth floor not being examined on Thursday. In that case, it places an unnecessary restriction on the seventh floor. (The sketch for the second question shows that the seventh floor could have been on Friday if the fourth floor was not on Thursday). And this offers no suggestion that the fourth floor couldn't be on Wednesday or Saturday. That eliminates **(D)**.

(E) also sets up an unhelpful conditional statement. If the third floor is examined on Thursday, it forces the fourth floor on Friday, which is what would have happened originally. However, what if the third floor is not examined on Thursday? Then, no restriction is placed on the fourth floor. It could potentially be placed on Saturday, which was not originally allowed. That eliminates **(E)**.

Glossary

Logical Reasoning

Logical Reasoning Question Types

Argument-Based Questions

Main Point Question

A question that asks for an argument's conclusion or an author's main point. Typical question stems:

> Which one of the following most accurately expresses the conclusion of the argument as a whole?

> Which one of the following sentences best expresses the main point of the scientist's argument?

Role of a Statement Question

A question that asks how a specific sentence, statement, or idea functions within an argument. Typical question stems:

> Which one of the following most accurately describes the role played in the argument by the statement that automation within the steel industry allowed steel mills to produce more steel with fewer workers?

> The claim that governmental transparency is a nation's primary defense against public-sector corruption figures in the argument in which one of the following ways?

Point at Issue Question

A question that asks you to identify the specific claim, statement, or recommendation about which two speakers/ authors disagree (or, rarely, about which they agree). Typical question stems:

> A point at issue between Tom and Jerry is

> The dialogue most strongly supports the claim that Marilyn and Billy disagree with each other about which one of the following?

Method of Argument Question

A question that asks you to describe an author's argumentative strategy. In other words, the correct answer describes *how* the author argues (not necessarily what the author says). Typical question stems:

> Which one of the following most accurately describes the technique of reasoning employed by the argument?

> Julian's argument proceeds by

> In the dialogue, Alexander responds to Abigail in which one of the following ways?

Parallel Reasoning Question

A question that asks you to identify the answer choice containing an argument that has the same logical structure and reaches the same type of conclusion as the argument in the stimulus does. Typical question stems:

> The pattern of reasoning in which one of the following arguments is most parallel to that in the argument above?

> The pattern of reasoning in which one of the following arguments is most similar to the pattern of reasoning in the argument above?

Assumption-Family Questions

Assumption Question

A question that asks you to identify one of the unstated premises in an author's argument. Assumption questions come in two varieties.

Necessary Assumption questions ask you to identify an unstated premise required for an argument's conclusion to follow logically from its evidence. Typical question stems:

> Which one of the following is an assumption on which the argument depends?

> Which one of the following is an assumption that the argument requires in order for its conclusion to be properly drawn?

Sufficient Assumption questions ask you to identify an unstated premise sufficient to establish the argument's conclusion on the basis of its evidence. Typical question stems:

> The conclusion follows logically if which one of the following is assumed?

> Which one of the following, if assumed, enables the conclusion above to be properly inferred?

Strengthen/Weaken Question

A question that asks you to identify a fact that, if true, would make the argument's conclusion more likely (Strengthen) or less likely (Weaken) to follow from its evidence. Typical question stems:

Strengthen

> Which one of the following, if true, most strengthens the argument above?

> Which one the following, if true, most strongly supports the claim above?

Weaken

Which one of the following, if true, would most weaken the argument above?

Which one of the following, if true, most calls into question the claim above?

Flaw Question

A question that asks you to describe the reasoning error that the author has made in an argument. Typical question stems:

The argument's reasoning is most vulnerable to criticism on the grounds that the argument

Which of the following identifies a reasoning error in the argument?

The reasoning in the correspondent's argument is questionable because the argument

Parallel Flaw Question

A question that asks you to identify the argument that contains the same error(s) in reasoning that the argument in the stimulus contains. Typical question stems:

The pattern of flawed reasoning exhibited by the argument above is most similar to that exhibited in which one of the following?

Which one of the following most closely parallels the questionable reasoning cited above?

Evaluate the Argument Question

A question that asks you to identify an issue or consideration relevant to the validity of an argument. Think of Evaluate questions as "Strengthen or Weaken" questions. The correct answer, if true, will strengthen the argument, and if false, will weaken the argument, or vice versa. Evaluate questions are very rare. Typical question stems:

Which one of the following would be most useful to know in order to evaluate the legitimacy of the professor's argument?

It would be most important to determine which one of the following in evaluating the argument?

Non-Argument Questions

Inference Question

A question that asks you to identify a statement that follows from the statements in the stimulus. It is very important to note the characteristics of the one correct and the four incorrect answers before evaluating the choices in Inference questions. Depending on the wording of the question stem,

the correct answer to an Inference question may be the one that

- *must be true* if the statements in the stimulus are true

- is *most strongly supported* by the statements in the stimulus

- *must be false* if the statements in the stimulus are true

Typical question stems:

If all of the statements above are true, then which one of the following must also be true?

Which one of the following can be properly inferred from the information above?

If the statements above are true, then each of the following could be true EXCEPT:

Which one of the following is most strongly supported by the information above?

The statements above, if true, most support which one of the following?

The facts described above provide the strongest evidence against which one of the following?

Paradox Question

A question that asks you to identify a fact that, if true, most helps to explain, resolve, or reconcile an apparent contradiction. Typical question stems:

Which one of the following, if true, most helps to explain how both studies' findings could be accurate?

Which one the following, if true, most helps to resolve the apparent conflict in the spokesperson's statements?

Each one of the following, if true, would contribute to an explanation of the apparent discrepancy in the information above EXCEPT:

Principle Questions

Principle Question

A question that asks you to identify corresponding cases and principles. Some Principle questions provide a principle in the stimulus and call for the answer choice describing a case that corresponds to the principle. Others provide a specific case in the stimulus and call for the answer containing a principle to which that case corresponds.

On the LSAT, Principle questions almost always mirror the skills rewarded by other Logical Reasoning question types. After each of the following Principle question stems, we note the question type it resembles. Typical question stems:

Which one of the following principles, if valid, most helps to justify the reasoning above? (**Strengthen**)

Which one of the following most accurately expresses the principle underlying the reasoning above? (**Assumption**)

The situation described above most closely conforms to which of the following generalizations? (**Inference**)

Which one of the following situations conforms most closely to the principle described above? (**Inference**)

Which one of the following principles, if valid, most helps to reconcile the apparent conflict among the prosecutor's claims? (**Paradox**)

Parallel Principle Question

A question that asks you to identify a specific case that illustrates the same principle that is illustrated by the case described in the stimulus. Typical question stem:

Of the following, which one illustrates a principle that is most similar to the principle illustrated by the passage?

Untangling the Stimulus

Conclusion Types

The conclusions in arguments found in the Logical Reasoning section of the LSAT tend to fall into one of six categories:

1) Value Judgment (an evaluative statement; e.g., Action X is unethical, or Y's recital was poorly sung)

2) "If"/Then (a conditional prediction, recommendation, or assertion; e.g., If X is true, then so is Y, or If you an M, then you should do N)

3) Prediction (X *will* or *will not* happen in the future)

4) Comparison (X is taller/shorter/more common/less common, etc. than Y)

5) Assertion of Fact (X is true or X is false)

6) Recommendation (we *should* or *should not* do X)

One-Sentence Test

A tactic used to identify the author's conclusion in an argument. Consider which sentence in the argument is the one the author would keep if asked to get rid of everything except her main point.

Subsidiary Conclusion

A conclusion following from one piece of evidence and then used by the author to support his overall conclusion or main point. Consider the following argument:

The pharmaceutical company's new experimental treatment did not succeed in clinical trials. As a result, the new treatment will not reach the market this year. Thus,

the company will fall short of its revenue forecasts for the year.

Here, the sentence "As a result, the new treatment will not reach the market this year" is a subsidiary conclusion. It follows from the evidence that the new treatment failed in clinical trials, and it provides evidence for the overall conclusion that the company will not meet its revenue projections.

Keyword(s) in Logical Reasoning

A word or phrase that helps you untangle a question's stimulus by indicating the logical structure of the argument or the author's point. Here are three categories of Keywords to which LSAT experts pay special attention in Logical Reasoning:

Conclusion words; e.g., *therefore, thus, so, as a result, it follows that, consequently,* [evidence] *is evidence that* [conclusion]

Evidence word; e.g., *because, since, after all, for,* [evidence] *is evidence that* [conclusion]

Contrast words; e.g., *but, however, while, despite, in spite of, on the other hand* (These are especially useful in Paradox and Inference questions.)

Experts use Keywords even more extensively in Reading Comprehension. Learn the Keywords associated with the Reading Comprehension section, and apply them to Logical Reasoning when they are helpful.

Mismatched Concepts

One of two patterns to which authors' assumptions conform in LSAT arguments. Mismatched Concepts describes the assumption in arguments in which terms or concepts in the conclusion are different *in kind* from those in the evidence. The author assumes that there is a logical relationship between the different terms. For example:

Bobby is a **championship swimmer**. Therefore, he **trains every day**.

Here, the words "trains every day" appear only in the conclusion, and the words "championship swimmer" appear only in the evidence. For the author to reach this conclusion from this evidence, he assumes that championship swimmers train every day.

Another example:

Susan does **not eat her vegetables**. Thus, she will **not grow big and strong**.

In this argument, not growing big and strong is found only in the conclusion while not eating vegetables is found only in the evidence. For the author to reach this conclusion from this evidence, she must assume that eating one's vegetables is necessary for one to grow big and strong.

See also Overlooked Possibilities.

Overlooked Possibilities

One of two patterns to which authors' assumptions conform in LSAT arguments. Overlooked Possibilities describes the assumption in arguments in which terms or concepts in the conclusion are different *in degree, scale, or level of certainty* from those in the evidence. The author assumes that there is no factor or explanation for the conclusion other than the one(s) offered in the evidence. For example:

> Samson does not have a ticket stub for this movie showing. Thus, Samson must have sneaked into the movie without paying.

The author assumes that there is no other explanation for Samson's lack of a ticket stub. The author overlooks several possibilities: e.g., Samson had a special pass for this showing of the movie; Samson dropped his ticket stub by accident or threw it away after entering the theater; someone else in Samson's party has all of the party members' ticket stubs in her pocket or handbag.

Another example:

> Jonah's marketing plan will save the company money. Therefore, the company should adopt Jonah's plan.

Here, the author makes a recommendation based on one advantage. The author assumes that the advantage is the company's only concern or that there are no disadvantages that could outweigh it, e.g., Jonah's plan might save money on marketing but not generate any new leads or customers; Jonah's plan might damage the company's image or reputation; Jonah's plan might include illegal false advertising. Whenever the author of an LSAT argument concludes with a recommendation or a prediction based on just a single fact in the evidence, that author is always overlooking many other possibilities.

See also Mismatched Concepts.

Causal Argument

An argument in which the author concludes or assumes that one thing causes another. The most common pattern on the LSAT is for the author to conclude that A causes B from evidence that A and B are correlated. For example:

> I notice that whenever the store has a poor sales month, employee tardiness is also higher that month. Therefore, it must be that employee tardiness causes the store to lose sales.

The author assumes that the correlation in the evidence indicates a causal relationship. These arguments are vulnerable to three types of overlooked possibilities:

1) There could be **another causal factor**. In the previous example, maybe the months in question are those in which the manager takes vacation, causing the store to lose sales and permitting employees to arrive late without fear of the boss's reprimands.

2) Causation could be **reversed**. Maybe in months when sales are down, employee morale suffers and tardiness increases as a result.

3) The correlation could be **coincidental**. Maybe the correlation between tardiness and the dip in sales is pure coincidence.

See also Flaw Types: Correlation versus Causation.

Another pattern in causal arguments (less frequent on the LSAT) involves the assumption that a particular causal mechanism is or is not involved in a causal relationship. For example:

> The airport has rerouted takeoffs and landings so that they will not create noise over the Sunnyside neighborhood. Thus, the recent drop in Sunnyside's property values cannot be explained by the neighborhood's proximity to the airport.

Here, the author assumes that the only way that the airport could be the cause of dropping property values is through noise pollution. The author overlooks any other possible mechanism (e.g., frequent traffic jams and congestion) through which proximity to the airport could be cause of Sunnyside's woes.

Principle

A broad, law-like rule, definition, or generalization that covers a variety of specific cases with defined attributes. To see how principles are treated on the LSAT, consider the following principle:

> It is immoral for a person for his own gain to mislead another person.

That principle would cover a specific case, such as a seller who lies about the quality of construction to get a higher price for his house. It would also correspond to the case of a teenager who, wishing to spend a night out on the town, tells his mom "I'm going over to Randy's house." He knows that his mom believes that he will be staying at Randy's house, when in fact, he and Randy will go out together.

That principle does not, however, cover cases in which someone lies solely for the purpose of making the other person feel better or in which one person inadvertently misleads the other through a mistake of fact.

Be careful not to apply your personal ethics or morals when analyzing the principles articulated on the test.

Flaw Types

Necessary versus Sufficient

This flaw occurs when a speaker or author concludes that one event is necessary for a second event from evidence that the first event is sufficient to bring about the second event, or vice versa. Example:

> If more than 25,000 users attempt to access the new app at the same time, the server will crash. Last night, at 11:15 PM, the server crashed, so it must be the case that more than 25,000 users were attempting to use the new app at that time.

In making this argument, the author assumes that the only thing that will cause the server to crash is the usage level (i.e., high usage is *necessary* for the server to crash). The evidence, however, says that high usage is one thing that will cause the server to crash (i.e., that high usage is *sufficient* to crash the server).

Correlation versus Causation

This flaw occurs when a speaker or author draws a conclusion that one thing causes another from evidence that the two things are correlated. Example:

> Over the past half century, global sugar consumption has tripled. That same time period has seen a surge in the rate of technological advancement worldwide. It follows that the increase in sugar consumption has caused the acceleration in technological advancement.

In any argument with this structure, the author is making three unwarranted assumptions. First, he assumes that there is no alternate cause, i.e., there is nothing else that has contributed to rapid technological advancement. Second, he assumes that the causation is not reversed, i.e., technological advancement has not contributed to the increase in sugar consumption, perhaps by making it easier to grow, refine, or transport sugar. And, third, he assumes that the two phenomena are not merely coincidental, i.e., that it is not just happenstance that global sugar consumption is up at the same time that the pace of technological advancement has accelerated.

Unrepresentative Sample

This flaw occurs when a speaker or author draws a conclusion about a group from evidence in which the sample cannot represent that group because the sample is too small or too selective, or is biased in some way. Example:

> Moviegoers in our town prefer action films and romantic comedies over other film genres. Last Friday, we sent reporters to survey moviegoers at several theaters in town, and nearly 90 percent of those surveyed were going to watch either an action film or a romantic comedy.

The author assumes that the survey was representative of the town's moviegoers, but there are several reasons to question that assumption. First, we don't know how many people were actually surveyed. Even if the number of people surveyed was adequate, we don't know how many other types of movies were playing. Finally, the author doesn't limit her conclusion to moviegoers on Friday nights. If the survey had been conducted at Sunday matinees, maybe most moviegoers would have been heading out to see an animated family film or a historical drama. Who knows?

Scope Shift/Unwarranted Assumption

This flaw occurs when a speaker's or author's evidence has a scope or has terms different enough from the scope or terms in his conclusion that it is doubtful that the evidence can support the conclusion. Example:

> A very small percentage of working adults in this country can correctly define collateralized debt obligation securities. Thus, sad to say, the majority of the nation's working adults cannot make prudent choices about how to invest their savings.

This speaker assumes that prudent investing requires the ability to accurately define a somewhat obscure financial term. But prudence is not the same thing as expertise, and the speaker does not offer any evidence that this knowledge of this particular term is related to wise investing.

Percent versus Number/Rate versus Number

This flaw occurs when a speaker or author draws a conclusion about real quantities from evidence about rates or percentages, or vice versa. Example:

> At the end of last season, Camp SunnyDay laid off half of their senior counselors and a quarter of their junior counselors. Thus, Camp SunnyDay must have more senior counselors than junior counselors.

The problem, of course, is that we don't know how many senior and junior counselors were on staff before the layoffs. If there were a total of 4 senior counselors and 20 junior counselors, then the camp would have laid off only 2 senior counselors while dismissing 5 junior counselors.

Equivocation

This flaw occurs when a speaker or author uses the same word in two different and incompatible ways. Example:

> Our opponent in the race has accused our candidate's staff members of behaving unprofessionally. But that's not

fair. Our staff is made up entirely of volunteers, not paid campaign workers.

The speaker interprets the opponent's use of the word *professional* to mean "paid," but the opponent likely meant something more along the lines of "mature, competent, and businesslike."

Ad Hominem

This flaw occurs when a speaker or author concludes that another person's claim or argument is invalid because that other person has a personal flaw or shortcoming. One common pattern is for the speaker or author to claim the other person acts hypocritically or that the other person's claim is made from self-interest. Example:

> Mrs. Smithers testified before the city council, stating that the speed limits on the residential streets near her home are dangerously high. But why should we give her claim any credence? The way she eats and exercises, she's not even looking out for her own health.

The author attempts to undermine Mrs. Smithers's testimony by attacking her character and habits. He doesn't offer any evidence that is relevant to her claim about speed limits.

Part versus Whole

This flaw occurs when a speaker or author concludes that a part or individual has a certain characteristic because the whole or the larger group has that characteristic, or vice versa. Example:

> Patient: I should have no problems taking the three drugs prescribed to me by my doctors. I looked them up, and none of the three is listed as having any major side effects.

Here, the patient is assuming that what is true of each of the drugs individually will be true of them when taken together. The patient's flaw is overlooking possible interactions that could cause problems not present when the drugs are taken separately.

Circular Reasoning

This flaw occurs when a speaker or author tries to prove a conclusion with evidence that is logically equivalent to the conclusion. Example:

> All those who run for office are prevaricators. To see this, just consider politicians: they all prevaricate.

Perhaps the author has tried to disguise the circular reasoning in this argument by exchanging the words "those who run for office" in the conclusion for "politicians" in the evidence, but all this argument amounts to is "Politicians prevaricate; therefore, politicians prevaricate." On the LSAT, circular

reasoning is very rarely the correct answer to a Flaw question, although it is regularly described in one of the wrong answers.

Question Strategies

Denial Test

A tactic for identifying the assumption *necessary* to an argument. When you negate an assumption necessary to an argument, the argument will fall apart. Negating an assumption that is not necessary to the argument will not invalidate the argument. Consider the following argument:

> Only high schools that produced a state champion athlete during the school year will be represented at the Governor's awards banquet. Therefore, McMurtry High School will be represented at the Governor's awards banquet.

Which one of the following is an assumption necessary to that argument?

> (1) McMurtry High School produced more state champion athletes than any other high school during the school year.

> (2) McMurtry High School produced at least one state champion athlete during the school year.

If you are at all confused about which of those two statements reflects the *necessary* assumption, negate them both.

> (1) McMurtry High School **did not produce more** state champion athletes than any other high school during the school year.

That does not invalidate the argument. McMurtry could still be represented at the Governor's banquet.

> (2) McMurtry High School **did not produce any** state champion athletes during the school year.

Here, negating the statement causes the argument to fall apart. Statement (2) is an assumption *necessary* to the argument.

Point at Issue "Decision Tree"

A tactic for evaluating the answer choices in Point at Issue questions. The correct answer is the only answer choice to which you can answer "Yes" to all three questions in the following diagram.

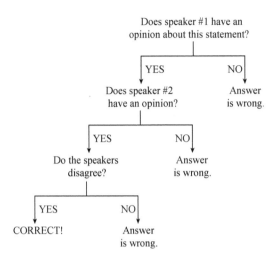

Common Methods of Argument

These methods of argument or argumentative strategies are common on the LSAT:

- Analogy, in which an author draws parallels between two unrelated (but purportedly similar) situations
- Example, in which an author cites a specific case or cases to justify a generalization
- Counterexample, in which an author seeks to discredit an opponent's argument by citing a specific case or cases that appear to invalidate the opponent's generalization
- Appeal to authority, in which an author cites an expert's claim or opinion as support for her conclusion
- Ad hominem attack, in which an author attacks her opponent's personal credibility rather than attacking the substance of her opponent's argument
- Elimination of alternatives, in which an author lists possibilities and discredits or rules out all but one
- Means/requirements, in which the author argues that something is needed to achieve a desired result

Wrong Answer Types in LR

Outside the Scope (Out of Scope; Beyond the Scope)

An answer choice containing a statement that is too broad, too narrow, or beyond the purview of the stimulus, making the statement in the choice irrelevant

180

An answer choice that directly contradicts what the correct answer must say (e.g., a choice that strengthens the argument in a Weaken question)

Extreme

An answer choice containing language too emphatic to be supported by the stimulus; often (although not always) characterized by words such as *all*, *never*, *every*, *only*, or *most*

Distortion

An answer choice that mentions details from the stimulus but mangles or misstates what the author said about those details

Irrelevant Comparison

An answer choice that compares two items or attributes in a way not germane to the author's argument or statements

Half-Right/Half-Wrong

An answer choice that begins correctly, but then contradicts or distorts the passage in its second part; this wrong answer type is more common in Reading Comprehension than it is in Logical Reasoning

Faulty Use of Detail

An answer choice that accurately states something from the stimulus, but does so in a manner that answers the question incorrectly; this wrong answer type is more common in Reading Comprehension than it is in Logical Reasoning

Logic Games

Game Types

Strict Sequencing Game

A game that asks you to arrange entities into numbered positions or into a set schedule (usually hours or days). Strict Sequencing is, by far, the most common game type on the LSAT. In the typical Strict Sequencing game, there is a one-to-one matchup of entities and positions, e.g., seven entities to be placed in seven positions, one per position, or six entities to be placed over six consecutive days, one entity per day.

From time to time, the LSAT will offer Strict Sequencing with more entities than positions (e.g., seven entities to be arranged over five days, with some days to receive more than one entity) or more positions than entities (e.g., six entities to be scheduled over seven days, with at least one day to receive no entities).

Other, less common variations on Strict Sequencing include:

Double Sequencing, in which each entity is placed or scheduled two times (there have been rare occurrences of Triple or Quadruple Sequencing). Alternatively, a Double Sequencing game may involve two different sets of entities each sequenced once.

Circular Sequencing, in which entities are arranged around a table or in a circular arrangement (NOTE: When the positions in a Circular Sequencing game are numbered, the first and last positions are adjacent.)

Vertical Sequencing, in which the positions are numbered from top to bottom or from bottom to top (as in the floors of a building)

Loose Sequencing Game

A game that asks you to arrange or schedule entities in order but provides no numbering or naming of the positions. The rules in Loose Sequencing give only the relative positions (earlier or later, higher or lower) between two entities or among three entities. Loose Sequencing games almost always provide that there will be no ties between entities in the rank, order, or position they take.

Circular Sequencing Game

See Strict Sequencing Game.

Selection Game

A game that asks you to choose or include some entities from the initial list of entities and to reject or exclude others. Some Selection games provide overall limitations on the number of entities to be selected (e.g., "choose exactly four of seven students" or "choose at least two of six entrees") while others provide little or no restriction on the number selected ("choose at least one type of flower" or "select from among seven board members").

Distribution Game

A game that asks you to break up the initial list of entities into two, three, or (very rarely) four groups or teams. In the vast majority of Distribution games, each entity is assigned to one and only one group or team. A relatively common variation on Distribution games will provide a subdivided list of entities (e.g., eight students—four men and four women—will form three study groups) and will then require representatives from those subdivisions on each team (e.g., each study group will have at least one of the men on it).

Matching Game

A game that asks you to match one or more members of one set of entities to specific members of another set of entities, or that asks you to match attributes or objects to a set of entities. Unlike Distribution games, in which each entity is placed in exactly one group or team, Matching games usually permit you to assign the same attribute or object to more than one entity.

In some cases, there are overall limitations on the number of entities that can be matched (e.g., "In a school's wood shop, there are four workstations—numbered 1 through 4—and each workstation has at least one and at most three of the following tools—band saw, dremmel tool, electric sander, and power drill"). In almost all Matching games, further restrictions on the number of entities that can be matched to a particular person or place will be found in the rules (e.g., Workstation 4 will have more tools than Workstation 2 has).

Hybrid Game

A game that asks you to do two (or rarely, three) of the standard actions (Sequencing, Selection, Distribution, and Matching) to a set of entities.

The most common Hybrid is Sequencing-Matching. A typical Sequencing-Matching Hybrid game might ask you to schedule six speakers at a conference to six one-hour speaking slots (from 9 AM to 2 PM), and then assign each speaker one of two subjects (economic development or trade policy).

Nearly as common as Sequencing-Matching is Distribution-Sequencing. A typical game of this type might ask you to divide six people in a talent competition into either a Dance category or a Singing category, and then rank the competitors in each category.

It is most common to see one Hybrid game in each Logic Games section, although there have been tests with two Hybrid games and tests with none. To determine the type of Hybrid you are faced with, identify the game's action in Step 1 of the Logic Games Method. For example, a game asking you to choose four of six runners, and then assign the four chosen runners to lanes numbered 1 through 4 on a track, would be a Selection-Sequencing Hybrid game.

Mapping Game

A game that provides you with a description of geographical locations and, typically, of the connections among them. Mapping games often ask you to determine the shortest possible routes between two locations or to account for the number of connections required to travel from one location to another. This game type is extremely rare, and as of February 2017, a Mapping game was last seen on PrepTest 40 administered in June 2003.

Process Game

A game that opens with an initial arrangement of entities (e.g., a starting sequence or grouping) and provides rules that describe the processes through which that arrangement can be altered. The questions typically ask you for acceptable arrangements or placements of particular entities after one, two, or three stages in the process. Occasionally, a Process game question might provide information about the arrangement after one, two, or three stages in the process and ask you what must have happened in the earlier stages. This game type is extremely rare, and as of November 2016, a Process game was last seen on PrepTest 16 administered in September 1995. However, there was a Process game on PrepTest 80, administered in December 2016, thus ending a 20-year hiatus.

Game Setups and Deductions

Floater

An entity that is not restricted by any rule or limitation in the game

Blocks of Entities

Two or more entities that are required by rule to be adjacent or separated by a set number of spaces (Sequencing games), to be placed together in the same group (Distribution games), to be matched to the same entity (Matching games), or to be selected or rejected together (Selection games)

Limited Options

Rules or restrictions that force all of a game's acceptable arrangements into two (or occasionally three) patterns

Established Entities

An entity required by rule to be placed in one space or assigned to one particular group throughout the entire game

Number Restrictions

Rules or limitations affecting the number of entities that may be placed into a group or space throughout the game

Duplications

Two or more rules that restrict a common entity. Usually, these rules can be combined to reach additional deductions. For example, if you know that B is placed earlier than A in a sequence and that C is placed earlier than B in that sequence, you can deduce that C is placed earlier than A in the sequence

and that there is at least one space (the space occupied by B) between C and A.

Master Sketch

The final sketch derived from the game's setup, rules, and deductions. LSAT experts preserve the Master Sketch for reference as they work through the questions. The Master Sketch does not include any conditions from New-"If" question stems.

Logic Games Question Types

Acceptability Question

A question in which the correct answer is an acceptable arrangement of all the entities relative to the spaces, groups, or selection criteria in the game. Answer these by using the rules to eliminate answer choices that violate the rules.

Partial Acceptability Question

A question in which the correct answer is an acceptable arrangement of some of the entities relative to some of the spaces, groups, or selection criteria in the game, and in which the arrangement of entities not included in the answer choices could be acceptable to the spaces, groups, or selection criteria not explicitly shown in the answer choices. Answer these the same way you would answer Acceptability questions, by using the rules to eliminate answer choices that explicitly or implicitly violate the rules.

Must Be True/False; Could Be True/False Question

A question in which the correct answer must be true, could be true, could be false, or must be false (depending on the question stem), and in which no additional rules or conditions are provided by the question stem

New-"If" Question

A question in which the stem provides an additional rule, condition, or restriction (applicable only to that question), and then asks what must/could be true/false as a result. LSAT experts typically handle New-"If" questions by copying the Master Sketch, adding the new restriction to the copy, and working out any additional deductions available as a result of the new restriction before evaluating the answer choices.

Rule Substitution Question

A question in which the correct answer is a rule that would have an impact identical to one of the game's original rules on the entities in the game

Rule Change Question

A question in which the stem alters one of the original rules in the game, and then asks what must/could be true/false as a result. LSAT experts typically handle Rule Change questions by reconstructing the game's sketch, but now accounting for the changed rule in place of the original. These questions are rare on recent tests.

Rule Suspension Question

A question in which the stem indicates that you should ignore one of the original rules in the game, and then asks what must/could be true/false as a result. LSAT experts typically handle Rule Suspension questions by reconstructing the game's sketch, but now accounting for the absent rule. These questions are very rare.

Complete and Accurate List Question

A question in which the correct answer is a list of any and all entities that could acceptably appear in a particular space or group, or a list of any and all spaces or groups in which a particular entity could appear

Completely Determine Question

A question in which the correct answer is a condition that would result in exactly one acceptable arrangement for all of the entities in the game

Supply the "If" Question

A question in which the correct answer is a condition that would guarantee a particular result stipulated in the question stem

Minimum/Maximum Question

A question in which the correct answer is the number corresponding to the fewest or greatest number of entities that could be selected (Selection), placed into a particular group (Distribution), or matched to a particular entity (Matching). Often, Minimum/Maximum questions begin with New-"If" conditions.

Earliest/Latest Question

A question in which the correct answer is the earliest or latest position in which an entity may acceptably be placed. Often, Earliest/Latest questions begin with New-"If" conditions.

"How Many" Question

A question in which the correct answer is the exact number of entities that may acceptably be placed into a particular group

or space. Often, "How Many" questions begin with New-"If" conditions.

Reading Comprehension

Strategic Reading

Roadmap

The test taker's markup of the passage text in Step 1 (Read the Passage Strategically) of the Reading Comprehension Method. To create helpful Roadmaps, LSAT experts circle or underline Keywords in the passage text and jot down brief, helpful notes or paragraph summaries in the margin of their test booklets.

Keyword(s) in Reading Comprehension

Words in the passage text that reveal the passage structure or the author's point of view and thus help test takers anticipate and research the questions that accompany the passage. LSAT experts pay attention to six categories of Keywords in Reading Comprehension:

Emphasis/Opinion—words that signal that the author finds a detail noteworthy or that the author has positive or negative opinion about a detail; any subjective or evaluative language on the author's part (e.g., *especially, crucial, unfortunately, disappointing, I suggest, it seems likely*)

Contrast—words indicating that the author finds two details or ideas incompatible or that the two details illustrate conflicting points (e.g., *but, yet, despite, on the other hand*)

Logic—words that indicate an argument, either the author's or someone else's; these include both Evidence and Conclusion Keywords(e.g., *thus, therefore, because, it follows that*)

Illustration—words indicating an example offered to clarify or support another point (e.g., *for example, this shows, to illustrate*)

Sequence/Chronology—words showing steps in a process or developments over time (e.g., *traditionally, in the past, today, first, second, finally, earlier, subsequent*)

Continuation—words indicating that a subsequent example or detail supports the same point or illustrates the same idea as the previous example (e.g., *moreover, in addition, also, further, along the same lines*)

Margin Notes

The brief notes or paragraph summaries that the test taker jots down next to the passage in the margin of the test booklet

Big Picture Summaries: Topic/Scope/Purpose/Main Idea

A test taker's mental summary of the passage as a whole made during Step 1 (Read the Passage Strategically) of the Reading Comprehension Method. LSAT experts account for four aspects of the passage in their big picture summaries:

Topic—the overall subject of the passage

Scope—the particular aspect of the Topic that the author focuses on

Purpose—the author's reason or motive for writing the passage (express this as a verb; e.g., *to refute, to outline, to evaluate, to critique*)

Main Idea—the author's conclusion or overall takeaway; if the passage does not contain an explicit conclusion or thesis, you can combine the author's Scope and Purpose to get a good sense of the Main Idea.

Passage Types

Kaplan categorizes Reading Comprehension passages in two ways, by subject matter and by passage structure.

Subject matter categories

In the majority of LSAT Reading Comprehension sections, there is one passage from each of the following subject matter categories:

Humanities—topics from art, music, literature, philosophy, etc.

Natural Science—topics from biology, astronomy, paleontology, physics, etc.

Social Science—topics from anthropology, history, sociology, psychology, etc.

Law—topics from constitutional law, international law, legal education, jurisprudence, etc.

Passage structure categories

The majority of LSAT Reading Comprehension passages correspond to one of the following descriptions. The first categories—Theory/Perspective and Event/Phenomenon—have been the most common on recent LSATs.

Theory/Perspective—The passage focuses on a thinker's theory or perspective on some aspect of the Topic; typically (though not always), the author disagrees and critiques the thinker's perspective and/or defends his own perspective.

Event/Phenomenon—The passage focuses on an event, a breakthrough development, or a problem that has recently arisen; when a solution to the problem is proposed, the author most often agrees with the solution (and that represents the passage's Main Idea).

Biography—The passage discusses something about a notable person; the aspect of the person's life emphasized by the author reflects the Scope of the passage.

Debate—The passage outlines two opposing positions (neither of which is the author's) on some aspect of the Topic; the author may side with one of the positions, may remain neutral, or may critique both. (This structure has been relatively rare on recent LSATs.)

Comparative Reading

A pair of passages (labeled Passage A and Passage B) that stand in place of the typical single passage exactly one time in each Reading Comprehension section administered since June 2007. The paired Comparative Reading passages share the same Topic, but may have different Scopes and Purposes. On most LSAT tests, a majority of the questions accompanying Comparative Reading passages require the test taker to compare or contrast ideas or details from both passages.

Question Strategies

Research Clues

A reference in a Reading Comprehension question stem to a word, phrase, or detail in the passage text, or to a particular line number or paragraph in the passage. LSAT experts recognize five kinds of research clues:

Line Reference—An LSAT expert researches around the referenced lines, looking for Keywords that indicate why the referenced details were included or how they were used by the author.

Paragraph Reference—An LSAT expert consults her passage Roadmap to see the paragraph's Scope and Purpose.

Quoted Text (often accompanied by a line reference)—An LSAT expert checks the context of the quoted term or phrase, asking what the author meant by it in the passage.

Proper Nouns—An LSAT expert checks the context of the person, place, or thing in the passage, asking whether the author made a positive, negative, or neutral evaluation of it and why the author included it in the passage.

Content Clues—These are terms, concepts, or ideas from the passage mentioned in the question stem but not as direct quotes and not accompanied by line references. An LSAT expert knows that content clues almost always refer to something that the author emphasized or about which the author expressed an opinion.

Reading Comp Question Types

Global Question

A question that asks for the Main Idea of the passage or for the author's primary Purpose in writing the passage. Typical question stems:

Which one of the following most accurately expresses the main point of the passage?

The primary purpose of the passage is to

Detail Question

A question that asks what the passage explicitly states about a detail. Typical question stems:

According to the passage, some critics have criticized Gilliam's films on the grounds that

The passage states that one role of a municipality's comptroller in budget decisions by the city council is to

The author identifies which one of the following as a commonly held but false preconception?

The passage contains sufficient information to answer which of the following questions?

Occasionally, the test will ask for a correct answer that contains a detail *not* stated in the passage:

The author attributes each of the following positions to the Federalists EXCEPT:

Inference Question

A question that asks for a statement that follows from or is based on the passage but that is not necessarily stated explicitly in the passage. Some Inference questions contain research clues. The following are typical Inference question stems containing research clues:

Based on the passage, the author would be most likely to agree with which one of the following statements about unified field theory?

The passage suggests which one of the following about the behavior of migratory water fowl?

Given the information in the passage, to which one of the following would radiocarbon dating techniques likely be applicable?

Other Inference questions lack research clues in the question stem. They may be evaluated using the test taker's Big Picture Summaries, or the answer choices may make it clear that the test taker should research a particular part of the passage text. The following are typical Inference question stems containing research clues:

It can be inferred from the passage that the author would be most likely to agree that

Which one of the following statements is most strongly supported by the passage?

Other Reading Comprehension question types categorized as Inference questions are Author's Attitude questions and Vocabulary-in-Context questions.

Logic Function Question

A question that asks why the author included a particular detail or reference in the passage or how the author used a particular detail or reference. Typical question stems:

The author of the passage mentions declining inner-city populations in the paragraph most likely in order to

The author's discussion of Rimbaud's travels in the Mediterranean (lines 23–28) functions primarily to

Which one of the following best expresses the function of the third paragraph in the passage?

Logic Reasoning Question

A question that asks the test taker to apply Logical Reasoning skills in relation to a Reading Comprehension passage. Logic Reasoning questions often mirror Strengthen or Parallel Reasoning questions, and occasionally mirror Method of Argument or Principle questions. Typical question stems:

Which one of the following, if true, would most strengthen the claim made by the author in the last sentence of the passage (lines 51–55)?

Which one of the following pairs of proposals is most closely analogous to the pair of studies discussed in the passage?

Author's Attitude Question

A question that asks for the author's opinion or point of view on the subject discussed in the passage or on a detail mentioned in the passage. Since the correct answer may follow from the passage without being explicitly stated in it, some Author's Attitude questions are characterized as a subset of Inference questions. Typical question stems:

The author's attitude toward the use of DNA evidence in the appeals by convicted felons is most accurately described as

The author's stance regarding monetarist economic theories can most accurately be described as one of

Vocabulary-in-Context Question

A question that asks how the author uses a word or phrase within the context of the passage. The word or phrase in question is always one with multiple meanings. Since the correct answer follows from its use in the passage, Vocabulary-in-Context questions are characterized as a subset of Inference questions. Typical question stems:

Which one of the following is closest in meaning to the word "citation" as it used in the second paragraph of the passage (line 18)?

In context, the word "enlightenment" (line 24) refers to

Wrong Answer Types in RC

Outside the Scope (Out of Scope; Beyond the Scope)

An answer choice containing a statement that is too broad, too narrow, or beyond the purview of the passage

180

An answer choice that directly contradicts what the correct answer must say

Extreme

An answer choice containing language too emphatic (e.g., *all*, *never*, *every*, *none*) to be supported by the passage

Distortion

An answer choice that mentions details or ideas from the passage but mangles or misstates what the author said about those details or ideas

Faulty Use of Detail

An answer choice that accurately states something from the passage but in a manner that incorrectly answers the question

Half-Right/Half-Wrong

An answer choice in which one clause follows from the passage while another clause contradicts or deviates from the passage

Contrapositive

The conditional statement logically equivalent to another conditional statement formed by reversing the order of and negating the terms in the original conditional statement. For example, reversing and negating the terms in this statement:

If   A   →   B

results in its contrapositive:

If   ~B   →   ~A

To form the contrapositive of conditional statements in which either the sufficient clause or the necessary clause has more than one term, you must also change the conjunction *and* to *or*, or vice versa. For example, reversing and negating the terms and changing *and* to *or* in this statement:

If   M   →   O AND P

results in its contrapositive:

If   ~O OR ~P   →   ~M

Formal Logic Terms

Conditional Statement ("If"-Then Statement)

A statement containing a sufficient clause and a necessary clause. Conditional statements can be described in Formal Logic shorthand as:

    If [*sufficient clause*]   → [*necessary clause*]

In some explanations, the LSAT expert may refer to the sufficient clause as the statement's "trigger" and to the necessary clause as the statement's result.

For more on how to interpret, describe, and use conditional statements on the LSAT, please refer to "A Note About Formal Logic on the LSAT" in this book's introduction.

CPSIA information can be obtained
at www.ICGtesting.com
Printed in the USA
BVHW051344070222
628293BV00013B/321

9 781506 237657